JESUS: SOCIAL REVOLUTIONARY?

Jesus:
Social Revolutionary?

Peter McVerry SJ

Published 2008 by
Veritas Publications
7/8 Lower Abbey Street
Dublin 1
Ireland

Email publications@veritas.ie
Website www.veritas.ie

ISBN 978-1-84730-110-9

10 9 8 7 6 5 4 3 2

Scripture references taken from the New Revised Standard Version Bible, copyright © 1989, Division of Christian Education of the National Council of the Churches in the USA

A catalogue record for this book is available from the British Library.

Cover design: Padhraig Nolan, Artisan Visual Communication
Printed in Ireland by ColourBooks Ltd.

Veritas books are printed on paper made from the wood pulp of managed forests. For every tree felled, at least one tree is planted, thereby renewing natural resources.

Contents

Preface

This book may seriously damage what is not infrequently considered to be Christian faith, lead you to a new sense of freedom, an increasing interest and wonder at the world around you, reveal to you a personal wealth that surpasses your wildest dreams, a wealth that no one can take from you, from which everyone can benefit, and which increases in value the more it is shared.

The title of this book, *Jesus: Social Revolutionary?*, in spite of the question mark, may already have prevented some readers from starting to read it. What we are pleased to call our 'orthodox belief and upbringing' has assured us that Jesus' Kingdom, as he told Pilate, 'is not of this world' and that God's Kingdom must never be confused with any earthly kingdom. Jesus is God and the Kingdom he preached is a 'spiritual', not an earthly kingdom. To call Jesus a 'revolutionary', even with a defensive question mark following, can seem to be verging on blasphemy. This crude misunderstanding of 'spiritual' turns Christianity into an abstraction, makes the incarnation seem like an unfortunate slip-up on God's part and preserves us in a self-righteousness that need not concern itself with our starving world, our threatened environment, our obscene expenditure on weapons of death.

Please do read this book. It communicates life, not just information. It comes from the heart of the author, the result of many years working, making friends with and enjoying the company of people spoken of by the Pharisees as 'the 'sinners and outcasts'.

Jesus' friends were in Palestine; Peter McVerry's are in Dublin.

This book is profound, clearly written, charming and challenging. Peter McVerry writes of himself, 'I am neither a theologian nor a scripture scholar'. True, he has no footnotes, nor pages of acknowledgement to other writers on Jesus. He also writes from the heart, but where his heart is, he applies his brain also and in terse prose he gets to the heart of the matter about God, ourselves, every other human being and all creation.

Here are some questions to read before you begin the book, questions you can keep returning to after you have read it. Notice the difference in your reaction to the questions before you read the book and afterwards.

Could it be that what we often consider to be the essence and practice of our faith in God is, in fact, a subtle way of keeping God out of the way, so that God does not interfere, upsetting our plans and proposing impractical and impossible ways of behaving? The Jewish writer on Mysticism, Martin Buber, a most spiritual man, once wrote 'Nothing so masks the face of God as religion'. How does that statement affect you after reading this book?

This is a most 'orthodox book' and desperately needed for our times when the greed of the minority threatens to choke the whole human race, while that same minority also threatens all human existence. In its fears of 'rogue nations' and of 'terrorism' and under the name of 'security', it already possesses many more nuclear weapons than would be needed to extinguish all life on earth. And Christians honour proponents of such destruction, called 'National Security', invite them to lecture and congratulate them on their wisdom!

Where is God? 'Nearer to you than you are to yourself.' In every human being we encounter. There are no exceptions, not even among our enemies! Creation itself is a sacrament of God. What is the most important moment of your life? It is the present moment, for God is always in the now. And what is this God like? God is compassionate to all creation. God's love is without limit; forgiveness is given even before we ask for it. God is the answer to the restlessness of our hearts, to our deepest longings.

Jesus identifies himself with us, whoever we are, whatever our background. All this and much more you will find in this book. It is a book to be pondered, prayed and lived. It will bring you a peace that cannot be taken from you. It will also bring you trouble, as Jesus foretold, but the joy of Jesus' company makes the burden light.

May this book be widely read and lead to economic, social and political change for the benefit of the whole human race and the greater glory of God!

Gerard W. Hughes SJ
author of God of Surprises

Introduction

Many understand Christianity to be a religion that imposes certain moral obligations on its followers – understood to be the will of God – which, if we observe them, will win us a place, after death, in the Kingdom of God. For them, Jesus was a teacher, who provided guidance for our moral lives. Christianity is thus seen as a *personal* code of morality, with love of neighbour, of course, at the centre.

> I give you a new commandment, that you
> love one another. Just as I have loved you,
> you also should love one another.
> (John 13:34)

> In everything do to others as you would
> have them do to you; for this is the law
> and the prophets. (Matthew 7:12)

> You shall love your neighbour as yourself.
> (Matthew 22:39)

Those, then, who are welcome into the Christian community, are those who are willing to live according to its moral norms. In this scenario, the distribution of wealth in our society and world, housing policy or budget decisions have little, if anything, to do with our following of Jesus in this community. The demands made on the members of this community are essentially moral, religious and personal, and not social, economic or political.

For others, often, but not exclusively, right-wing evangelical Christians, Christianity is a religion whereby if we 'believe in' Jesus, we will, after death, be given a place in the Kingdom of God. 'Believing in' can easily become 'believing that' Jesus is the Son of God, the Saviour, the Truth, the Way etc. 'Believing in' comes to be understood as believing a set of facts about Jesus. Thus those who are welcome into the Christian community are those who are willing to affirm a set of beliefs about who Jesus was and is.

Here again, social, economic or political reform is irrelevant, or at least very marginal, to our following of Jesus, which is essentially a personal relationship with Jesus based on our belief in who he is.

Of course, these are not two totally divergent views of Christianity. Although the focus of each view is different, there is considerable overlap between them. Accepting the moral obligations of the Gospel involves believing in Jesus as Saviour, while accepting Jesus as Saviour has certain consequences for our behaviour.

However, they both emphasise a view of the Gospel and the Christian community as essentially involving personal belief and/or inter-personal moral obligations, with little or no economic, social or political consequences.

Both views see Jesus' message as primarily about heaven and how to get there. Both views understand Christianity as inherently individualistic. Community becomes a gathering together of like-minded individuals who share a common belief or commit themselves to a common moral code. The invitation of Jesus to individuals, then, is not essentially an invitation to community, and the commitment of individuals is not essentially a commitment to community, but rather to a belief system or moral code. Community tends to become a support structure, rather like a club or society that has common interests and objectives.

For me, both views present a major problem – they both fail to explain the death of Jesus. Certainly, they both agree that Jesus died and rose again. They both explain *why* Jesus died – if Jesus' message is about heaven and how to get there, then Jesus died for us, in order to make forgiveness possible, which is the prerequisite for entering heaven.

Both avoid explaining *how* Jesus died. Jesus didn't die in bed of old age! After at most three years of public ministry – and more likely only nine months – Jesus was put to death by the religious/political leaders of his day. And not just put to death, but crucified. To understand the mission and ministry of Jesus, and therefore the mission and ministry of his followers, we have to explain *why Jesus was crucified*.

Jesus was not put to death by bad guys who couldn't stand a good guy. They were sincere and devout people who believed they were doing God's will.

Jesus was not put to death because his moral demands were at variance with those of the Jewish faith of his time. A person does not get executed for telling people to be kind, be nice, be good.

Nor was he put to death because he demanded to be recognised as the Son of God – the Christian community only understood this *after* Jesus' death. To understand the meaning of the Christian faith, and the consequences of believing in Jesus for his followers, we have to explain not just *that* Jesus died, not just *why* Jesus died, but also *how* he died, *the manner* of his death.

This book is an attempt to find an answer to these questions: Why was Jesus put to death, by crucifixion, by the religious/political authorities of his day? What was Jesus doing or saying that was so threatening to them that they felt they had to take this action? What are the implications of this for the followers of Jesus and for the life and ministry of the Christian community?

I am neither a theologian nor a scripture scholar. Theologians and scripture scholars who read this book will probably agree! The understanding of God and of the life and ministry of Jesus presented in this book is shaped largely by my work with homeless young people. They have revealed to me who God is, much more than all my theology lectures. (My theology lecturers would argue that that is due to my frequent absences from class!)

They have opened up the scriptures to me in a wonderfully enriching way.

I offer this book as an attempt, in the context of an Ireland which has become unbelievably rich but where many feel uncomfortable at the levels of homelessness and poverty that continue to exist in our society, to open a debate about the meaning of our faith and the obligations that belonging to the Christian community imposes on us. It suggests that Jesus was put to death by good people, acting for good reasons, because the God that Jesus revealed had radical consequences for the ordering, behaviour and structures of society, consequences that threatened the existing order of society. It suggests that Jesus was crucified because the leaders of his time understood that the economic, social and political consequences of the personal transformation that comes from becoming a disciple of Jesus were revolutionary. The religious authorities believed that the society they lived in was ordered according to the will of God and they were acting in accordance with the will of God in handing Jesus over to be executed. The Gospels describe a clash between two very different understandings of God, with two radically different implications for our personal lives and for the structuring of our world. Jesus lost and died; but he, his understanding of God and his vision for our world were vindicated by the Resurrection.

2   Jesus and the Outcasts

Jesus and the Marginalised

Reading the Gospels for the first time I think what is most striking about the life of Jesus is that, again and again, he healed the
sick, associated with 'undesirables' and ate with social outcasts.

Stories of Jesus healing people abound.

> They went to Capernaum; and when the
> sabbath came, he entered the synagogue
> and taught. They were astounded at his
> teaching, for he taught them as one hav-
> ing authority, and not as the scribes. Just
> then there was in their synagogue a man
> with an unclean spirit, and he cried out,
> 'What have you to do with us, Jesus of
> Nazareth? Have you come to destroy us?
> I know who you are, the Holy One of God.'
> But Jesus rebuked him, saying, 'Be silent,
> and come out of him!' And the unclean
> spirit, convulsing him and crying with a
> loud voice, came out of him. They were all
> amazed, and they kept on asking one
> another, 'What is this? A new teaching –
> with authority! He commands even the
> unclean spirits, and they obey him.' At
> once his fame began to spread through-
> out the surrounding region of Galilee.

As soon as they left the synagogue, they entered the house of Simon and Andrew, with James and John. Now Simon's mother-in-law was in bed with a fever, and they told him about her at once. He came and took her by the hand and lifted her up. Then the fever left her, and she began to serve them.

That evening, at sundown, they brought to him all who were sick or possessed with demons. And the whole city was gathered around the door. And he cured many who were sick with various diseases, and cast out many demons; and he would not permit the demons to speak, because they knew him.

(Mark 1:21-34)

Again and again, the religious authorities were scandalised by his association with outcasts, particularly by his eating with them, which was a sign of respect, friendship and acceptance. In the culture of Jesus' time, sharing a meal was more than just about food – it was a form of social inclusion; while refusing to share a meal was a form of social exclusion. Meals reflected the social boundaries of a group.

Jesus went out again beside the sea; the whole crowd gathered around him, and he taught them. As he was walking along, he saw Levi son of Alphaeus sitting at the tax booth, and he said to him, 'Follow me.' And he got up and followed him.

And as he sat at dinner in Levi's house, many tax collectors and sinners were also sitting with Jesus and his disciples – for there were many who followed him. When the scribes of the Pharisees saw that he was eating with sinners and tax collectors, they said to his disciples, 'Why does he eat with tax collectors and sinners?' When Jesus heard this, he said to them, 'Those who are well have no need of a physician, but those who are sick; I have come to call not the righteous but sinners.'

(Mark 2:13-17)

All who saw it [Jesus inviting himself to a meal at Zacchaeus' house] began to grumble and said, 'He has gone to be the guest of one who is a sinner.'

(Luke 19:7)

For John came neither eating nor drinking, and they say, 'He has a demon'; the Son of Man came eating and drinking, and they say, 'Look, a glutton and a drunkard, a friend of tax collectors and sinners!'

(Matthew 11:18-19)

In the story of the life of Jesus, there were three groups to whom he reached out in a preferential way:

1. The sick, the lame, the blind, the deaf, the dumb – those who were afflicted with some infirmity.

2. The poor – the majority of the population of Israel, whose life was hard and who struggled to make ends meet, many of whom survived from day to day.

3. Public sinners, notably tax collectors and prostitutes.

What these three groups had in common was the attitude of society towards them and the way they were treated by the society in which they lived. They were all despised, looked down upon, treated as second-class citizens, not wanted, kept at arm's length.

They shared this attitude for different reasons:

- The infirm were looked down upon because it was believed that they (or their parents) had committed some sin and they were therefore being punished by God. God was angry with them; they were no friends of God. And so, those in society who were righteous believed that if the infirm were out of favour with God, then they should also be out of favour with God's friends. They were, therefore, consigned to the margins of their society.

  > As Jesus walked along, he saw a man blind from birth. His disciples asked him, 'Rabbi, who sinned, this man or his parents, that he was born blind?' (John 9:1-2)

- Similarly, the poor were despised because they didn't keep the Law. They didn't keep the Law because they didn't know the Law. The Law, by the time of Jesus, had become complicated, consisting of thousands of minute prescriptions governing every aspect of everyday life. Some of these rules are described in the Gospels.

  > At that time Jesus went through the grain fields on the sabbath; his disciples were hungry, and they began to pluck heads of grain and to eat. When the Pharisees saw it, they said to him, 'Look, your disciples are doing what is not lawful to do on the sabbath.' (Matthew 12:1-2)

Now when the Pharisees and some of the scribes who had come from Jerusalem gathered around him, they noticed that some of his disciples were eating with defiled hands, that is, without washing them. (For the Pharisees, and all the Jews, do not eat unless they thoroughly wash their hands, thus observing the tradition of the elders; and they do not eat anything from the market unless they wash it; and there are also many other traditions that they observe, the washing of cups, pots and bronze kettles.) So the Pharisees and the scribes asked him, 'Why do your disciples not live according to the tradition of the elders, but eat with defiled hands?'

(Mark 7:1-6)

In order to know the complex details of the Law you had to study the Law. To study the Law, you had to have the education and money to do so. The poor had neither and so could not know the Law or keep the Law in all its detail. But because observance of the Law was the primary demand and desire of God, then, again, the poor were not in God's favour and so were outcast by God's people.

Then the temple police went back to the chief priests and Pharisees, who asked them, 'Why did you not arrest him?' The police answered, 'Never has anyone spoken like this!' Then the Pharisees replied, 'Surely you have not been deceived too, have you? Has any one of the authorities or of the Pharisees believed in him? But this crowd, which does not know the law – they are accursed.' (John 7:45-49)

- Public sinners, tax collectors and prostitutes were despised because of their way of life. God could not possibly want anything to do with them. Therefore God's friends should want nothing to do with them either.

> Two men went up to the temple to pray, one a Pharisee and the other a tax collector. The Pharisee, standing by himself, was praying thus, 'God, I thank you that I am not like other people: thieves, rogues, adulterers, or even like this tax collector. I fast twice a week; I give a tenth of all my income.' (Luke 18:9-12)

The groups that Jesus preferentially reached out to had in common that they were all marginalised in the society to which they belonged. They were marginalised because their society believed that God had also marginalised them. The attitudes of society towards them and the way society treated them ensured that they were kept apart, at arm's length.

Dignity

But why did Jesus reach out to these groups in a preferential sort of way? Perhaps it has to do with *dignity*. One way of summing up the whole revelation of Jesus is to say that, as God is the parent of us all, every human being has the same dignity of being a child of God, no matter who we are or what we may have done.

When Jesus found someone whose dignity as a human being, a child of God, was being undermined or denied by the attitudes of society and the way in which they were treated, then he had to respond, if he was to be true to the revelation of God that he came to bring. And he responded in three different ways:

He affirmed their dignity by the way in which he himself related to them. By reaching out to them in a respectful and dignified way, he communicated to them a sense of their own dignity, in the face of the contrary message that they were continually receiving from society. It was as if he said to them: 'Society may not want much to do with you, society may look down on you, but I, and the God from whom I come, we acknowledge your dignity, the same dignity as any other human being in this society.'

He challenged the attitudes of the society that looked down upon such people, and he challenged the structures that kept them in their marginalised place.

Thus he challenged the attitude of Simon, who showed himself to be embarrassed and offended by the presence of a woman who was a sinner and came into his house to wash the feet of Jesus and dry them with her hair.

> One of the Pharisees asked Jesus to eat with him, and he went into the Pharisee's house and took his place at the table. And a woman in the city, who was a sinner, having learned that he was eating in the Pharisee's house, brought an alabaster jar of ointment. She stood behind him at his feet, weeping, and began to bathe his feet with her tears and to dry them with her hair. Then she continued kissing his feet and anointing them with the ointment. Now when the Pharisee who had invited him saw it, he said to himself, 'If this man were a prophet, he would have known who and what kind of woman this is who is touching him - that she is a sinner.' Jesus spoke up and said to him, 'Simon, I have something to say to you.' 'Teacher," he replied, 'Speak.' 'A certain creditor had two debtors; one owed five hundred denarii, and the other fifty. When they could not pay, he cancelled the debts for both of them. Now which of them will love him more?"

Simon answered, 'I suppose the one for whom he cancelled the greater debt.' And Jesus said to him, "You have judged rightly." Then turning toward the woman, he said to Simon, "Do you see this woman? I entered your house; you gave me no water for my feet, but she has bathed my feet with her tears and dried them with her hair. You gave me no kiss, but from the time I came in she has not stopped kissing my feet. You did not anoint my head with oil, but she has anointed my feet with ointment. There-fore, I tell you, her sins, which were many, have been forgiven; hence she has shown great love. But the one to whom little is forgiven, loves little.' Then he said to her, "Your sins are forgiven.' But those who were at the table with him began to say among themselves, 'Who is this who even forgives sins?' And he said to the woman, 'your faith has saved you; go in peace.' (Luke 7:36-50)

He broke the Law, and supported his disciples who broke the Law, when that Law did not allow him to reach out in compassion.

Now he was teaching in one of the syna-gogues on the sabbath. And just then there appeared a woman with a spirit that had crippled her for eighteen years. She was bent over and was quite unable to stand up straight. When Jesus saw her, he called her over and said, 'Woman, you are set free from your ailment.' When he laid his hands on her, immediately she stood

up straight and began praising God. But
the leader of the synagogue, indignant
because Jesus had cured on the sabbath,
kept saying to the crowd, 'There are six
days on which work ought to be done;
come on those days and be cured, and
not on the sabbath day.' But the Lord
answered him and said, 'You hypocrites!
Does not each of you on the sabbath untie
his ox or his donkey from the manger, and
lead it away to give it water? And ought
not this woman, a daughter of Abraham
whom Satan bound for eighteen long
years, be set free from this bondage on
the sabbath day?'

(Luke 13:10-16)

The third way in which Jesus affirmed the dignity of those on the
margins of his own society was not of his own choice. It was
imposed on him. *His affirmation of their dignity, by his own association with them, led Jesus himself to become marginalised.* This was,
in fact, the ultimate affirmation of their dignity. As the opposition from the religious authorities grew, and Jesus, too, came to
be rejected and pushed to the margins, he did not pull back or
change his mind but continued, even to death, to stand up for
and accompany those who were despised.

A Political Act

The challenge that Jesus posed by eating with sinners lay in the
simple, but deeply profound, act of looking at a human being
whom society considered of little value, of little use, of little worth
and recognising that person's extraordinary dignity as a child of
God – indeed, as we shall see, recognising their privileged place
in the mind and heart of God. That simple, God-like act of reaching out and caring for someone whom most people considered of
no value reflected God's vision of humanity and the compassion

of God. In reaching out to them, Jesus revealed the nature of
and, in doing so, fulfilled the mission that God had given to l

But it was not just Jesus' choice of company that anno,
and alienated the religious authorities. Why did this apparently
simple act of compassion bring out the anger and hostility of the
religious authorities? Why did they find it so threatening?

The religious authorities, in their conventional wisdom,
believed that excluding the poor, the sinner and the tax collector
was the right and moral thing to do. It was what God was asking
of them. That conventional wisdom believed that those who,
through their sinfulness, had made themselves enemies of God
had to be rejected and set apart from the People of God. In sin-
ning, they had defiled the Covenant that God had made with the
people. It is difficult for us to appreciate the enormous significance of this. Conventional religious belief held that holiness
consisted in separation from all that is unholy, impure. If the
People of God failed to exclude these sinners, the People of God
would become, like them, impure. Then the wrath of God would
be visited on the whole People of God, and the unique relationship that the Covenant created between the Chosen People and
God would be at risk, and therefore Israel's very existence as a
nation, which was founded on that Covenant, would be in jeopardy.

It seems to me that only one person in the Gospels understood the significance of what Jesus was doing. It wasn't any of
the Apostles, or his mother, or any of the women who followed
Jesus – it was Caiphas, the High Priest, when he said:

> It is better that one man should die than
> the nation perish. (John 11:50)

You didn't have to be a prophet to foresee that Jesus' fellowship with
those whom his society wished to exclude would lead to his death.

'Jesus ate with tax collectors and sinners.' This simple act of
friendship was at the same time a profoundly political act. And
Jesus knew it. And the religious leaders knew it. It led to a confrontation between them, and Jesus lost. The crucifixion was

another political act, the inevitable consequence of that political act of eating with tax collectors and sinners.

Ireland Today

The poor, then, are those groups who, in our societies, are pushed aside, unwanted, rejected, marginalised. We can identify them with the question: 'Who do you not want living beside you?'

Living the Gospel is to affirm the dignity of every human being as a child of God. Affirming the dignity of travellers, homeless people, drug users and offenders is often a challenge to the conventional thinking of a society that feels insecure and often afraid, and so wants to keep them apart, at arm's length. The more we have to protect, the stronger the tendency to insulate ourselves from those on the margins whom we may perceive as a threat to our security. Thus, although prosperous to a degree that we could never have dreamt of a decade ago, there are more homeless people on our streets than ever before, our prisons are more crowded, hospital waiting lists are longer. There is less tolerance for those with addictions, mental health problems, personality disorders and the adult effects of child sexual abuse.

Affirming the dignity of those on the margins today may also be a profoundly political act, just as it was in Jesus' time. It may involve a challenge to the political authorities if they fail to provide for their basic needs. Caring, today, is often a political act.

We are sometimes told that religion and politics should be kept apart, but that was not Jesus' way. His caring and insistence on the dignity of every person as a child of God had political implications for the ordering of his own society – and still has today for the ordering of our own society. It also had personal implications for himself and his life, turning many of his contemporaries against him and mobilising the authorities to get rid of him. So, too, our caring may demand political changes in our own society and may also have personal implications for our own lives.

3 Who is God?

I believe that Jesus came to tell us only one thing: who God is. He didn't come to tell us anything about the past or the future, about heaven or hell, just who God is. That was Jesus' charism: he had come from God, he knew God intimately as Son of God and he came to reveal that God to us – God's yearning, God's desire, God's passion.

The Kingdom of God

To tell us who God is, Jesus talked about the Kingdom of God. God and God's Kingdom were at the centre of Jesus' life and ministry.

- At the beginning of his ministry, Jesus announced that the Kingdom of God was at hand.

   > From that time [when Jesus heard that John had been arrested] Jesus began to proclaim, 'Repent, for the kingdom of heaven has come near.' (Matthew 4:17)

- Throughout his ministry, Jesus talked about the Kingdom of God (the Jews tried to avoid using the word 'God' and often substituted the word 'heaven' for it).

   > He put before them another parable: 'The kingdom of heaven is like a mustard seed

that someone took and sowed in his field;
it is the smallest of all the seeds, but when
it has grown it is the greatest of shrubs and
becomes a tree, so that the birds of the air
come and make nests in its branches.'

He told them another parable: 'The
kingdom of heaven is like yeast that a
woman took and mixed in with three
measures of flour until all of it was leav-
ened.' (Matthew 13:31-33)

He put before them another parable: 'The
kingdom of heaven may be compared to
someone who sowed good seed in his
field ...' (Matthew 13:24)

- At the end of his ministry, Jesus does not deny the accusa-
  tion made against him that the Kingdom of God has come
  in his own person.

Now Jesus stood before the governor;
and the governor asked him, 'Are you the
King of the Jews?' Jesus said, 'You say so.'
(Matthew 27:11)

The Kingdom of God (heaven) was a common topic of con-
versation amongst the Jews. That was, after all, the very *raison
d'être* of the Jewish people – they were chosen to inherit the
Kingdom of God. They awaited the coming of the Messiah to
lead them into the Kingdom. Before the coming of Jesus there
were many false Messiahs who proclaimed the coming of the
Kingdom, and no doubt after Jesus there were many more false
Messiahs proclaiming the coming of the Kingdom. So when
Jesus came, saying, 'The Kingdom of God is at hand', I suspect
the Jewish people said to themselves: 'Here we go again, another
one!'

But Jesus said two things about the Kingdom of God – and therefore about who God is – that were new and radical.

Entry into the Kingdom of God – Compassion

The first was in answer to the question: 'How do I enter the Kingdom of God?' This was a key question, indeed the most fundamental question, for every Jew, as God had offered the Kingdom to them. Jewish theology had its answer: Entry into the Kingdom of God is through observance of the Law.

For the Jews, then, observance of the Law was the most important obligation in their life. When the Jewish people were called and chosen by God, God gave them the Law through Moses. God entered into a covenant with them, whereby God promised to be their God, to protect them and to lead them into the Kingdom of God, *provided* the Jewish people, in turn, observed the Law that God was giving them that day. So observance of the Law in all its detail was the primary obligation imposed on every Jew, the proof of their fidelity to God and the gate through which they would enter into that Kingdom God had promised them. For Jewish theology, God's passion was the observance of the Law.

So when Jesus came along and said that entry into the Kingdom of God was *not* through observance of the Law, the religious authorities were horrified. Jesus was undermining the very foundations of Judaism. If they followed what Jesus was saying, the wrath of God would be visited upon a disobedient people.

So if Jesus declared that entry into the Kingdom of God was *not* through observance of the Law, how did one enter the Kingdom?

For Jesus there was only one gate by which we could enter into the Kingdom of God – and that gate was *compassion*. The following three passages from the Gospels illustrate this.

LAST JUDGEMENT SCENE (MATTHEW 25:31-46)
The story of the Last Judgement is an extremely important story for Matthew. We know that for two reasons. First, it is the

very last story in Matthew's Gospel before the passion narrative. Matthew places this story there to emphasise it is the climax of his Gospel, the whole of his Gospel is leading up to this story as its crescendo, its apex. Second, Matthew introduces the story by painting a picture of great solemnity. He does this to alert his listeners to the fact that what is coming next is very important. Matthew begins the story with:

> When the Son of Man comes in his glory,
> and all the angels with him, then he will sit
> on the throne of his glory. All the nations
> will be gathered before him.
>
> (Matthew 25:31)

And what do we read in Matthew's story?

> Come, you that are blessed by my Father,
> inherit the kingdom prepared for you from
> the foundation of the world; for I was hun-
> gry and you gave me food, I was thirsty
> and you gave me something to drink, I
> was a stranger and you welcomed me,
> I was naked and you gave me clothing, I
> was sick and you took care of me, I was in
> prison and you visited me.
>
> (Matthew 25:34-36)

The message is clear: entry into the Kingdom of God is through compassion.

THE RICH MAN AND LAZARUS (LUKE 16:19-22)
In this story, Jesus tells us about a rich man. Interestingly, he tells us nothing about the rich man's life, or indeed spiritual life, except that he was rich. He doesn't tell us whether he was a good Jew or not, whether he went to the synagogue on the sabbath or not, whether he prayed or not, whether he observed the Law or

not. Instead, he just paints a picture of a rich man for his listeners to imagine:

> There was a rich man who was dressed in
> purple and fine linen and who feasted
> sumptuously every day. (Luke 16:19)

Why does Luke tell us nothing about the rich man's life, or spiritual life, except that he was rich? Perhaps because it was irrelevant – *if* he had failed in the one thing that is most important to God, namely compassion. Not that the rich man's life, or spiritual life, was irrelevant, full stop. No, but it *becomes* irrelevant if he fails in the one thing that is most important to God, namely compassion.

Luke tells us about a poor man. Again, interestingly, he tells us nothing about the poor man, except that he was poor. He paints a picture of poverty for his listeners to imagine:

> And at his gate lay a poor man named
> Lazarus, covered with sores, who longed
> to satisfy his hunger with what fell from
> the rich man's table; even the dogs would
> come and lick his sores. (Luke 16:20-21)

In particular, he doesn't bother telling us how he became poor – maybe he drank all his money, maybe he gambled it or maybe, like the prodigal son, he squandered it on the good life. Why does Luke not tell us how he became poor? Perhaps, again, because it was irrelevant. For Luke, and God, there is no distinction between the deserving poor and the undeserving poor.

The story concerns a child of God in need (how he came to be in need was irrelevant) and another child of God who could have reached out and met that need but failed to do so. And for that, there was no place for him in the Kingdom of God.

The Good Samaritan (Luke 10:25-37)

The Good Samaritan is a story that is very familiar to most of us – perhaps too familiar! I don't believe that it is a story just encouraging us to be good neighbours to each other. If so, then any child in Sixth Class with a good creative spirit might have thought up this story.

No, the story of the Good Samaritan begins with two questions. The most immediate is, of course, the question: 'Who is my neighbour?' But there is a prior question, asked by a lawyer:

> Teacher what must I do to inherit eternal
> life?

The story of the Good Samaritan is the answer to *that* question. In the story, Luke describes two people who came across a man lying on the side of the road, robbed and beaten. They both passed by on the other side. Why does Luke pick a priest and a Levite as the two characters to pass by? Were they just the first two role models that came into his head? Hardly. Luke composes his stories very carefully. Luke chooses the priest and the Levite precisely because they observed the Law. They considered themselves righteous and were looked up to by the rest of society as righteous precisely because of their observance of the Law. They were considered close to God, friends of God, in God's favour. But for Jesus, there was no place for them in the Kingdom of God because they had failed in compassion.

The third person, the one who would be welcomed into the Kingdom of God? If we were part of the group listening to Jesus telling the story, we might say to ourselves: 'We can understand Jesus picking the priest and the Levite – always a little anti-clerical Jesus was!' But the third person, the one who will make it, who will it be? I know: it will be a good Jewish layperson.

And then Jesus came out with 'A Samaritan'. You can hear a gasp from the audience: a Samaritan! The most despised of people by the Jews. And why? Despised precisely because they did not obey the Law, they did not believe in the God who gave the Law through Moses, they were considered to be worshipping a false God. So how could God want anything to do with a Samaritan. They were no friends of God. Yet it was a Samaritan whom Jesus said was going to be welcomed into the Kingdom of God, because of his compassion.

Just then a lawyer stood up to test Jesus. 'Teacher,' he said, 'what must I do to inherit eternal life?' He said to him, 'What is written in the law? What do you read there?' He answered, 'You shall love the Lord your God with all your heart, and with all your soul, and with all your strength, and with all your mind; and your neighbour as yourself.' And he said to him, 'You have given the right answer; do this, and you will live.'

But wanting to justify himself, he asked Jesus, 'And who is my neighbour?' Jesus replied, 'A man was going down from Jerusalem to Jericho, and fell into the hands of robbers, who stripped him, beat him and went away, leaving him half dead. Now by chance a priest was going down that road; and when he saw him, he passed by on the other side. So likewise a Levite, when he came to the place and saw him, passed by on the other side. But a Samaritan while travelling came near him; and when he saw him, he was moved with pity. He went to him and bandaged his wounds, having poured oil and wine on them. Then he put him on his own animal, brought him to an inn, and took care of him. The next day he took out two denarii, gave them to the innkeeper, and said, 'Take care of him; and when I come back, I will repay you whatever more you spend.' Which of these three, do you think, was a neighbour to the man who fell into the hands of the robbers?' He said, 'The one who showed him mercy.' Jesus said to him, 'Go and do likewise.'

Exclusion from the Kingdom of God – Doing Nothing

Just as Jesus announced that entry into the Kingdom of God was through compassion, so he warned us that ignoring the suffering of those around us would exclude us from the Kingdom of God.

LAST JUDGEMENT SCENE REVISITED

In the Last Judgement Scene, Jesus, the Son of Man returns in glory, turns to those on his left and says:

> You that are accursed, depart from me into the eternal fire prepared for the devil and his angels; for I was hungry and you gave me no food, I was thirsty and you gave me nothing to drink, I was a stranger and you did not welcome me, naked and you did not give me clothing, sick and in prison and you did not visit me.
>
> (Matthew 26:41-43)

Now, Jesus in the Gospels is always portrayed as the one who forgives, who makes excuses for people, who never condemns. So what had they done to merit such condemnation from one who never condemns?

The answer was nothing – they had done absolutely nothing. 'I was hungry and you did absolutely nothing, I was thirsty and you did absolutely nothing – depart from me you cursed.'

The Rich Man and Lazarus Revisited

In the story of the rich man and Lazarus, I always had a great sympathy for the rich man: after all, it wasn't his fault that Lazarus lay at his gate. Maybe it was the poor man's own fault; or maybe it was 'the structures', but it wasn't the rich man's fault. But he was excluded from the Kingdom of God, not because he was personally responsible for the plight of Lazarus, but because he did absolutely nothing.

The Good Samaritan Revisited

In the Good Samaritan story, if Jesus had stood at the gates of Jericho when the priest and the Levite arrived, and called them over and said to them, 'Do you know that you did something so terrible on that journey that there can be no place for you in the Kingdom of God?' they wouldn't have known what Jesus was talking about. They would have scratched their heads and thought: 'What did I do wrong? Didn't rob the parish finances. Didn't run off with the parish secretary. There was just that dead body by the side of the road.' And for that, there was no place for them in the Kingdom of God.

The Kingdom of God as Metaphor

It is important to mention here that Jesus was not trying to tell us anything about heaven or hell or who goes there. Jesus' mission and message were not about an afterlife, but about life in this world. The point of the stories is to tell us who God is, what is important to God in the here and now. Jesus uses a concept that was so central to the life and concern of the Jews, namely entry into and exclusion from the Kingdom of God, to try to communicate to us who God is, what is God's passion.

And Jesus tells us that God's passion is God's children, not the observance of the Law. Like any parent, God is passionate about the children, with a special concern for those children who are suffering. God is so grateful to us when we reach out to one of God's children who is suffering and try to take some of that suffering off their shoulders that God promises us everything that God can give us, namely the Kingdom of God. And God is so pained when we simply ignore the suffering of God's children that the only image Jesus can find to express to the Jews how deeply pained God is, is the image of exclusion from the Kingdom that has been promised to them.

The God of Compassion v the God of the Law

It was clear to the Jewish authorities that Jesus was threatening the very basis of their faith. He was undermining the faith of the people in the true God (the God-whose-passion-is-the-observance-of-the-Law) and inventing a different God (the God-whose-passion-is-compassion). He was therefore not only seen as an enemy of the Jewish faith and nation, he was an enemy of the true God, an ally of Satan.

> Then they brought to him a demoniac who was blind and mute; and he cured him, so that the one who had been mute could speak and see. All the crowds were amazed and said, 'Can this be the Son of David?' But when the Pharisees heard it, they said, 'It is only by Beelzebub, the ruler of the demons, that this fellow casts out the demons.'
>
> (Matthew 12:22-24)

WHO WILL BE IN THE KINGDOM OF GOD?

But for the religious authorities, it was to get worse – much worse. The second question that Jesus answered in a new and radical way was one that was even harder for them to swallow. The question was: Who shall be in the Kingdom of God?

Again, Jewish theology had an answer. If entry into the Kingdom of God was through observance of the Law, then those who observed the Law would obviously be in the Kingdom; and the better you observed the Law, then the higher your place would be in the Kingdom.

Now, who observed the Law? As stated earlier, the Law was so complex by the time of Jesus, that in order to know the Law, you had to study it. And to study the Law, you needed the money and education to do so. So who knew the Law? Why, the Pharisees, the scribes, the lawyers, the priests, those who were wealthy and powerful in Israel. The poor didn't know the Law in all its detail, so they were unable to observe the Law in all its detail. Hence the conventional wisdom was that the Pharisees, scribes, lawyers and priests would be there in the highest places in the Kingdom, but the poor – if they got in at all, which was very unlikely! – would be down in the basement. So when Jesus came along and told the Pharisees

> Truly I tell you, the tax collectors and pros-
> titutes are making their way into the
> Kingdom of God ahead of you
> (Matthew 21:31)

that didn't win him too many friends in high places!

In answer to the question, 'Who shall be in the Kingdom of God?' Jesus answered, 'The Kingdom belongs to the poor.'

The Kingdom belongs to the Poor

Again, I choose three well-known passages from the Gospels to illustrate.

THE STORY OF THE WEDDING FEAST (LUKE 14:7-24)

Luke tells us that Jesus was invited to a feast by one of the leaders of the Pharisees – not any old Pharisee, mind you, but one of the leading Pharisees! As the meal got under way, we are reminded that the most important guests made sure that they got the places of honour, as was the custom. So when the meal was over, and Jesus, as the invited guest, was asked to give his after-dinner speech, he tells them:

When you are invited by someone to a
wedding banquet, do not sit down at the
place of honour, in case someone more
distinguished than you has been invited
by your host; and the host who invited
both of you may come and say to you,
'Give this person your place,' and then in
disgrace you would start to take the lowest place. (Luke 14:8-9)

You can imagine the guests being embarrassed. Possibly what
Jesus describes may actually have happened and some very hon-
oured guest was, to their great shame, seated in the lowest place.
You can imagine them whispering to each other: 'Who does he
think he is? We give him a fine meal – it looks as if he hasn't
eaten for days – and then he turns around and insults us.'

When Jesus is finished addressing the guests, he turns to his
host and says: 'When you give a feast, don't invite this shower' –
or words to that effect!

When you give a luncheon or a dinner, do
not invite your friends or your brothers or
your relatives or rich neighbours, in case
they may invite you in return, and you
would be repaid. But when you give a
banquet, invite the poor, the crippled, the
lame and the blind. And you will be
blessed, because they cannot repay you,
for you will be repaid at the resurrection
of the righteous. (Luke 14:12-14)

Then someone speaks up from amongst the guests, to ask:

Who shall be in the Kingdom of God?

Jesus tells the story of the wedding feast – when the day comes, all who were invited make their excuses. The person giving the feast got angry and sent his servants out into the streets of the town to bring in 'the poor, the crippled, the blind and the lame', exactly the same people that he urged his host to invite to his own feast. In answer to the guest's question, 'Who shall be in the Kingdom of God?' Jesus answers, 'The poor, the crippled, the lame and the blind.'

But there is still room. So Jesus sends out his servants again but this time says, 'compel them to come in'. I always wondered: What about their civil rights? If they don't want to come in, is it right to compel them to come in?

The analogy I would use to understand this instruction of Jesus is that of a homeless person wandering the lanes of a country road close to a small town, all his belongings in a plastic Tesco bag. And in that town, in a magnificent mansion on the top of the hill, lives a very wealthy and important man. Along comes a servant from the mansion, who says to the homeless person: 'The master up there in that big house is giving a party tonight, and he has sent me especially to invite you.' What do you think would be the reaction of the homeless person? 'Come off it, you're having me on, you're playing a joke at my expense. The guy up in that house wouldn't want the likes of me there. I'll go up with you, and everyone will be looking at me and laughing, and I'll be kicked out as soon as I get in. No way, there's no way I'm going up there.'

At the time of Jesus, the poor did not believe that there would be a place for them in the Kingdom of God. So Jesus says, 'Go out, *compel* them to come in. It is only when they are in, and eating from the feast, that they will then realise, it really was true, the Kingdom is for us.'

> Then Jesus said to him, 'Someone gave a
> great dinner and invited many. At the
> time for the dinner he sent his slave to say
> to those who had been invited, "Come; for

everything is ready now." But they all alike began to make excuses. The first said to him, "I have bought a piece of land, and I must go out and see it; please accept my regrets." Another said, "I have bought five yoke of oxen, and I am going to try them out; please accept my regrets." Another said, "I have just been married, and therefore I cannot come." So the slave returned and reported this to his master. Then the owner of the house became angry and said to his slave, "Go out at once into the streets and lanes of the town and bring in the poor, the crippled, the blind and the lame." And the slave said, "Sir, what you ordered has been done and there is still room." Then the master said to the slave, "Go out into the roads and lanes, and compel people to come in, so that my house may be filled. For I tell you, none of those who were invited will taste my dinner."' (Luke 14:16-24)

At the feast in the Kingdom will be the poor, the crippled, the lame and the blind, those who were rejected and despised by their society.

Jesus' First Sermon (Luke 4:16-21)
The very first words that Jesus utters in Luke's Gospel are intended by Luke to be a summary of Jesus' whole mission. Those first words are:

When he came to Nazareth, where he had been brought up, he went to the synagogue on the sabbath day, as was his custom. He stood up to read, and the scroll of the prophet Isaiah was given to him. He unrolled the scroll and found the place where it was written: 'The Spirit of the Lord is upon me, because he has anointed me to bring good news to the poor. He has sent me to proclaim release to the captives and recovery of sight to the blind, to let the oppressed go free, to proclaim the year of the Lord's favour.' And he rolled up the scroll, gave it back to the attendant and sat down. The eyes of all in the synagogue were fixed on him. Then he began to say to them, 'Today this scripture has been fulfilled in your hearing.'

Jesus came to bring the Good News to the poor. What was that good news? That the Kingdom of God belonged to them.

THE BEATITUDES (LUKE 6:17-26)
That the Kingdom belonged to the poor was a very radical teaching of Jesus. So in case we have any doubts, Luke gives us the Beatitudes, the constitution of the community that he was inaugurating. All commentators agree that Luke's Beatitudes are closer to the original words of Jesus than Matthew's Beatitudes: Matthew adapts them to meet the needs of the particular group whom he was addressing.

And what do Luke's Beatitudes say?

Then he looked up at his disciples and said: 'Blessed are you who are poor, for yours is the kingdom of God.'

The Kingdom of Jesus v Kingdom of Institutional Religion
So the kingdom that Jesus revealed was radically different in two ways from the Kingdom that the Jewish authorities believed in:

- Entry into that Kingdom was through compassion and there was no other gate by which you could enter.
- The Kingdom belonged, not to the righteous who kept the Law, but to the poor.

The God that Jesus revealed was also, therefore, radically different in two ways from the God of Jewish theology:

- God is passionate about God's children, particularly those who are suffering; the Law was intended to teach us how to relate to God and to one another in compassion, but it was not meant to be an end in itself. God is not particularly interested in whether we observe all the details of the Law or not – and certainly not at the expense of compassion.
- God has a special place in God's heart for those who are poor, excluded, unwanted and rejected. They, too, are God's children and the way they are treated pains God immensely. In the Kingdom, God's justice will be done.

JESUS IS QUESTIONED BY THE PHARISEES

Now, when my time is over and I arrive (hopefully) at the gates of heaven, I will have one question for God: 'If it is so important for us to believe in you, why did you make it so difficult? Could you not, now and again, have given us a little sign that you exist? Maybe you could have gone around the rivers of Ireland, say once a year, and done a little parting of the waters so that everyone could cross over, and then people would be able to say, "Yes, now • I know God exists; I have seen the sign."'

How will God reply? I think I know what God will say, because the Jewish authorities asked him the same question.

THE PHARISEES ASK FOR A SIGN

When Jesus came with this radically different understanding of God and God's Kingdom than the Jews expected, naturally they asked him for a sign that he was speaking the truth from God. But Jesus refused.

> The Pharisees came and began to argue
> with him, asking him for a sign from
> heaven, to test him. And he sighed deeply
> in his spirit and said, 'Why does this gen-
> eration ask for a sign? Truly I tell you, no
> sign will be given to this generation.'
>
> (Mark 8:11-12)

I always thought that was a little unreasonable of Jesus – the least
he could have done was to give them a sign. So what is going on
here?

Like myself at the gates of heaven, the Pharisees were asking for a miraculous sign:

> Others, to test him, kept demanding
> from him a sign from heaven.
>
> (Luke 11:16)

But Jesus knew that miracles prove nothing – every generation
has its magicians!

JOHN THE BAPTIST ASKS FOR A SIGN
In fact, Jesus was giving them signs all along, but they couldn't
recognise them. One person asked for a sign and got it – John the
Baptist.

> The disciples of John reported all these
> things to him. So John summoned two of
> his disciples and sent them to the Lord to
> ask, 'Are you the one who is to come, or
> are we to wait for another?' When the
> men had come to him, they said, 'John
> the Baptist has sent us to you to ask, "Are
> you the one who is to come, or are we to
> wait for another?"' Jesus had just then
> cured many people of diseases, plagues

and evil spirits, and had given sight to
many who were blind. And he answered
them, 'Go and tell John what you have
seen and heard: the blind receive their
sight, the lame walk, the lepers are
cleansed, the deaf hear, the dead are
raised, the poor have good news brought
to them. And blessed is anyone who takes
no offence at me.' (Matthew 7:18-23)

THE ONLY TRUE SIGNS

The signs that Jesus was from God were the signs of compassion.
When you look at a little baby in the pram, you say (at least if the
parents are listening): 'Oh, isn't he gorgeous – the image of his
father' (or mother – depending on which parent is present!). How
do you know that the child is the child of the parent? Because you
recognise in the child the same features that you see in the parent.

Jesus was trying to say something similar: God is compassion; therefore you can only recognise the Son of God by the
Son's compassion. And if you cannot recognise, by my compassion, that I have come from God, then you do not know God.

And if God is compassion, and you can only know the Son
of God by the Son's compassion, you can only know the disciple
of God by the disciple's compassion.

> By this shall all know that you are my dis-
> ciples, by your love for one another.
> (John 13:35)

This is what identifies us as a follower of Jesus. The central
requirement in the teaching of Jesus is:

> Be compassionate as your Heavenly Father
> is compassionate. (Matthew 5:48)

So what will God say to me, then, at those gates of heaven?

'When your faith grew dim, where should you have gone to have your faith restored? Not to the river bank to observe some miraculous sign. No, you should have looked at the countless acts of compassion, at the small, hidden efforts of countless people reaching out to the sick, the lonely, the depressed, the unwanted, and *there* you would have found the evidence that I, who am compassion, exist.'

The Last Judgement

When I was going to school, I was made to believe that at the Last Judgement, McVerry would have to stand up there in front of everyone and all his sins would be read out and the few good things he did would be read out, and the weighing scales would be produced to see if I deserved to get into the Kingdom or not. And after McVerry, then Joe Bloggs would have to get up and then John Doe and so on. I think that after the first few hundred thousand, it's going to get very boring!

So maybe the Last Judgement is not about the revelation of McVerry, or anyone else, to the world but maybe it is God's final revelation to the world of who God is. Here we have the whole world gathered before God and now, finally, once and for all, God reveals who God is.

And who is God? God is compassion. So what better way of revealing that God is compassion than by ushering into the Kingdom all those who were made to suffer here on earth, all those who were unwanted, rejected, cast out, despised. They enter the Kingdom of God, not because they lived better lives than the rest of us, not because they were more moral than the rest of us – but because God is compassion.

And the rest of us? We will be left scratching our heads and wondering if we, too, might get in. We will get in if we have made friends with the poor. If we have reached out to the poor and tried to relieve their pain, then they will turn around and invite us into *their* Kingdom. If we have simply ignored the poor, then how can we expect them to invite us into their Kingdom?

They will – through forgiveness. But that's for another chapter.

Ireland Today

When I was growing up, the Catholic Church was a Church of the Law. You were identified as a good Catholic by your adherence to a variety of laws and regulations: going to Mass on Sunday, not eating meat on Friday, fasting during Lent, not getting a divorce, not using artificial contraceptives and so on. Your fidelity to the Church's laws and rules was the proof of your fidelity to God. A Church that proposes fidelity to laws is, wittingly or unwittingly, transmitting a particular understanding of God, namely a God-whose-passion-is-observance-of-the-law.

The dominant image of God, then, is that of Judge. Our relationship to God is defined by our observance of laws – if we do as we are supposed to do, then God is pleased with us and will reward us; if we do not do as we are supposed to do, then God will be angry and punish us. Thus, *our relationship with God is controlled by us,* by our behaviour. In this respect, the Church had travelled down the same cul-de-sac that religion at the time of Jesus had once travelled. While the emphasis on observance of law as the criterion for our fidelity to God has diminished somewhat in recent years, nevertheless it remains the dominant emphasis for many people who have grown up within the Church.

Jesus sought to teach people a different image of God, God not as Judge, but God as Compassion – a God whose love for us is unchanging, whose forgiveness is greater than all our sinfulness, whose passion is compassion.

In Ireland today, despite the extraordinary wealth we have created, one in nine children lives in consistent poverty; that is to say, their families do not have enough money to feed them properly, to clothe them properly or to heat their homes properly. There are more homeless people than there were before the Celtic Tiger began. There·are more people on social housing waiting lists than before the Celtic Tiger began. There are children whose development is undermined by the lack of services available or the long waiting lists for assessment and treatment. There are still travellers living on the side of the road, often denied suitable accommodation by the refusal of the settled community to allow them access to housing or serviced sites.

Jesus' understanding of God is clear: the suffering, exclusion and rejection of the children of God is God's primary concern. Our prayer, our worship, our fasting are of little value to God if we have ignored those of God's children who suffer on the margins of our societies. We are Christians who follow the message of Jesus, not because we say 'Lord, Lord', but because we do what the Lord has asked of us. God is so grateful to us for everything we do to those of God's children who suffer that 'even the cup of cold water, given to the least of my brothers and sisters, will not go without its reward'. It is in our compassion that we imitate the God who is compassion; it is through our compassion that we grow into the image and likeness of God.

Many parents, today, tell me of their concern that their children have drifted away from the Church. They worry that they no longer go to Mass, no longer accept the Church's teachings and therefore have somehow abandoned God. But then they often add: 'But they are really good children, they would do anything for anybody.' I tell them not to worry. The kindness, the concern of their children for others does not go unnoticed by God. In their concern and compassion, they are close to God. They have not abandoned God and God has not abandoned them. They may have drifted away from the institutional Church, but their relationship with God is not to be identified with their relationship with the institutional Church. Indeed, these young people may have a prophetic message for us that we are not hearing: perhaps they are drifting away from the institutional Church because they no longer find God there.

4   Where is God to be Found?

When I get up to the gates of heaven, there is another issue that I have with God! Christians, Jews, Hindus, Muslims and many other religions all believe in God but they all have different ideas about who God is, different understandings of God. You would think that if it is so important for us human beings to understand God, that God would have made it very clear who God is. Instead, trying to understand God is like doing a very difficult crossword! ⁻

The Night Sky

Imagine two little children looking up at the stars on a very dark, clear night. One child says:

'I bet you those stars are five miles away.'

The other says:

'No, they're not – they're ten miles away.'

The first child says: 'Don't be stupid. If they were ten miles away you wouldn't be able to see them.'

'Course you'd be able to see them. There are no corners or anything in space, you eejit.'

'Who are you calling an eejit? I'm no eejit. You're the eejit, you just can't admit you're wrong.'

Thump, thump, fight breaks out.

These two children are, of course, correct in thinking that the stars are a very long way away. In their minds, five miles or ten miles are concepts that express the fact that the stars are a very long way away. However, five miles or ten miles are hopelessly inadequate concepts to express how far away the stars really are. But they are the only concepts the children have and *to them* they are expressing the truth. The concept that *would* adequately express the reality of the stars' location – 'quadrillions of miles away' – is beyond their comprehension.

Our little human minds and human concepts are incapable of understanding God. God is infinitely beyond human understanding. When we say that God is wise, beautiful or compassionate, we are ascribing to God concepts that take their meaning from our human experience. To understand what we mean when we say that God is compassion, we look at Mother Teresa. Or we look at my neighbour who cared for his disabled wife for thirty years, each day washing her, changing her, feeding her, without a single day's break. When we say that God is compassion, we say that God is like Mother Teresa or like my neighbour. And indeed that gives us some understanding of what God's compassion is like.

However, God's compassion is so infinitely greater than Mother Teresa's compassion or my neighbour's compassion; the word 'compassion', which describes Mother Teresa or my neighbour, in no way describes God. It tells us something about God that is true, yet it is a concept that is hopelessly inadequate to express that truth.

God is beyond our understanding. But we make the mistake of trying to 'capture' God within our puny little concepts and we claim that we know God, and believe that everyone who disagrees with us is wrong. We can never *know* God, we can only *search* for God. Searching for God is to acknowledge that we have not found God; that we have not understood God. Once we stop searching, we are in danger of claiming that we have found God, that we now understand God. And then we miss God.

So it is not exactly correct to say, as I did in the last chapter, that Jesus came to tell us *who God is* – not because Jesus did not know who God is, but because we cannot understand who God is. Perhaps Jesus could only tell us *where to find God.*

To Enter the Kingdom of God is to Find God

What do we mean by 'entering into the Kingdom of God'? We mean, of course, to 'find salvation'. The Kingdom of God is that place or state where, finally, we find our salvation.

What do we mean by 'finding salvation'? We mean 'finding God'. To find salvation is to enter into the presence of God for all eternity.

Hence:

> To enter into the Kingdom of God = to find salvation
> To find salvation = to find God

Therefore:

> To enter into the Kingdom of God = to find God

In those Gospel passages where Jesus talks about entering into the Kingdom of God through compassion, we usually understand Jesus to mean that if we show compassion to the poor and suffering *now*, when we *later* go before God for judgement, God will invite us into the Kingdom. But Jesus understood the Kingdom of God to mean not just a Kingdom in some afterlife, but also a Kingdom here and now. Jesus came to inaugurate the Kingdom of God on earth, just as it is in heaven.

From that perspective, then, when Jesus says, in the Last Judgement Scene,

> I was hungry and you gave me to eat ...
> inherit the kingdom prepared for you
> from the foundation of the world
> (Matthew 25:34-35)

we can understand it to mean 'I was hungry and you gave me to eat ... *at that moment*, you entered into the presence of God, you found God'. You find God in the hungry, the thirsty, the sick, the naked, those in prison. In the very act of reaching out to them, you discover God.

Hence those in the Last Judgement Scene, on the left, who suffer the condemnation of Jesus, are not being punished by

God for failing to have compassion for the poor. No, Jesus is simply stating a reality: 'I was hungry and you failed to recognise me, you failed to find God there; I was thirsty and you failed to recognise me, to find God there ...'

Again, in the story of the Rich Man and Lazarus, Jesus portrays the rich man as being excluded from the Kingdom of God. From this perspective, we can understand Jesus as saying: 'Despite your good acts, and your prayers and your attendance at the synagogue and your observance of the Law, God was present in the poor man sitting at your gate – and you failed to recognise God and find God there.' Hence the rich man has excluded himself from the presence of God, from salvation, from the Kingdom.

Similarly, in the Good Samaritan, the Priest and the Levite, despite their righteousness, failed to recognise and find God in the man, robbed and beaten, at the side of the road. God did not exclude them from the Kingdom because of their failing in compassion – no, they simply missed the Kingdom when they passed by on the other side. God's salvation was there to be found on the side of the road – and they missed it.

To Search for God

Perhaps we cannot even say that Jesus came to tell us where to find God. *We* cannot find God, God finds us. It might be more accurate to say that Jesus told us where to *search* for God. If we search for God where God is to be found, then God will reveal himself to us.

Of course, the religious tradition that Jesus grew up in was strong on the need for compassion, at least compassion for some. But Jesus' insistence that we search for God amongst the poor, the outcast and the suffering was completely unacceptable to that tradition. It was not just a theological debate between Jesus and the religious authorities – it cut to the very core of the Jewish faith.

GOD IS PRESENT ONLY IN THE TEMPLE

In that tradition, God was only to be found in one place: in the Holy of Holies, in the midst of the Temple in Jerusalem.

When the Jewish nation was wandering through the desert, God accompanied them, present in the Ark of the Covenant. It was more or less a tent on wheels, but that was God's home where one could go to find God.

When the chosen people settled down in the territory given them by God and they built houses for themselves in which to live, they also built God a house. That house, the house of God, was known as the Temple and it was located in Jerusalem. The Temple was the very centre of the Jewish faith. To be in the Temple was to be in God's presence in a very special way.

On feast days, Jewish pilgrims made their way up to Jerusalem, to the Temple, with great rejoicing:

> I was glad when they said to me,
> 'Let us go to the house of the Lord!'
> Our feet are standing
> within your gates, O Jerusalem.
> (Psalm 122:1-2)

> Now the Passover of the Jews was near, and many went up from the country to Jerusalem before the Passover to purify themselves. (John 11:55)

ARCHITECTURE OF TEMPLE –
HOLINESS AS SEPARATION FROM SINNERS

In the centre of that Temple was the Holy of Holies, that place where God resided. No one could enter the Holy of Holies except the priest, and then only on one day of the year, the day of Atonement. Present in the Holy of Holies, God was separated from God's people. Jewish theology understood God's holiness to consist in God's separation from all that is not holy. God was holy and therefore could not associate with sin or sinners or the impure. So God was isolated in the Holy of Holies, kept apart, protected from all that is not holy, including us human beings.

Around the Holy of Holies was an area where only the priests could enter – they were the holiest of the people and therefore the closest to God.

Outside the Priestly area, there was another area where the Jewish people were permitted to enter, Jewish men in one court-yard, Jewish women in another. They were forbidden to enter the area reserved for the priests.

And outside the area permitted to the Jewish people, further-most from God, there was an area that was open to the Gentiles, the least holy of all. They were forbidden to enter the area reserved for Jews.

Hence the architecture of the Temple reflected varying degrees of holiness: holiness consisted in separation from all that was less holy.

HOLINESS AS PROXIMITY TO SINNERS

Jesus announced a God who was not separated from God's peo-ple. Far from it: God was to be found there in the sick, the poor, the blind, the lame, the man robbed and beaten. God *identified* with the people. For Jesus, holiness consisted not in separation from sinners but in proximity to sinners.

How can one explain how upsetting this was for the religious authorities? For them, the Temple was where you found God. Since the priests were in that area closest to God, if people wished to approach God, they had to do so through the priests. Access to God was through the priests and only through the priests.

But Jesus declared that the people could find God, in their midst, in the poor and the suffering. They had no need to go to the Temple or go through the priests. 'Sacred space', where God is to be found, is not in the Temple but in the streets, the market-place, in people's homes. 'Sacred space' is the table around which you share a meal in fellowship, welcome and respect for the poor, the sinner, the infirm – and in that 'sacred space' you find God.

For the religious authorities, this was blasphemy: an insult to God, a rejection of the God who resided in the Temple.

JESUS DISTANCES HIMSELF FROM THE TEMPLE

The Beginning of Jesus' Life

Luke's Gospel describes the changing relationship of Jesus to the Temple. At the beginning, Jesus' life revolved around the Temple:

- the good news was first proclaimed in the Temple to Zechariah;
- when Jesus was born, Joseph and Mary brought him to the Temple for the ceremony of purification;
- Jesus, as an infant, was welcomed into the Temple by Simeon and Anna;
- when Jesus disappeared at twelve years of age, his parents found him in the Temple.

The story of Jesus begins with a very positive relationship to the Temple.

The End of Jesus' Life

Luke's Gospel ends very differently – Jesus in confrontation with the Temple:

- Jesus drives out the buyers and sellers from the Temple;
- he criticises the Temple authorities;
- he is arrested by the Temple police;
- he is tried by the Temple priests;
- he is handed over by the Temple authorities to be executed:

> Then they came to Jerusalem. And he entered the temple and began to drive out those who were selling and those who were buying in the temple, and he over-turned the tables of the money changers and the seats of those who sold doves;

and he would not allow anyone to carry anything through the temple. He was teaching and saying, 'Is it not written, "My house shall be called a house of prayer for all the nations"? But you have made it a den of robbers.' (Mark 11:15-17)

In casting out the buyers and sellers from the Temple, Jesus tells us why he does it: 'You have made it [the Temple] a den of robbers.' Here Jesus is associating himself with the criticism of the prophet Jeremiah:

Do not trust in these deceptive words: 'This is the temple of the Lord, the temple of the Lord, the temple of the Lord.' For if you truly amend your ways and your doings, if you truly act justly one with another, if you do not oppress the alien, the orphan and the widow, or shed innocent blood in this place, and if you do not go after other gods to your own hurt, then I will dwell with you in this place, in the land that I gave of old to your ancestors forever and ever.

Here you are, trusting in deceptive words to no avail. Will you steal, murder, commit adultery, swear falsely, make offerings to Baal and go after other gods that you have not known and then come and stand before me in this house, which is called by my name, and say, 'We are safe!' – only to go on doing all these abominations?

Has this house, which is called by my name, become a den of robbers in your sight? You know, I too am watching, says the Lord. (Jeremiah 7:4-11)

Jeremiah warns the religious leaders of his time that putting their faith in the Temple when they are failing to do justice is to deceive themselves. In this dramatic act, Jesus identifies with that prophetic understanding of God.

Jesus is subsequently arrested by the Temple police, tried and convicted by the Temple priests and handed over by the Temple authorities to be executed.

The story of Jesus is a story of a religious leader who came to dissociate himself from the Temple; in its place, he associated with the enemies of the Temple – sinners, tax collectors and prostitutes: he ate with them and joined with them in fellowship and welcome. He declared that God was amongst them, not in the Temple. Not surprisingly, therefore, he was rejected by the Temple, in the name of God.

The Final Act

The early Christian community understood that Jesus had rejected the Temple. At the moment of his death, Matthew, using symbolic images, describes the curtain of the Temple, which separated God in the Holy of Holies from all those who were outside, as being torn in two. Jesus' death was the final act in breaking down the separation of God from the people.

> At that moment the curtain of the temple
> was torn in two, from top to bottom.
> (Matthew 27:51)

Ireland Today

We often measure fidelity to the Church by Church attendance. Surveys regularly tell us what percentage of people in Ireland attend Mass, and the considerable reduction in that number is often understood to be an indicator of the drift towards a more Godless society. The Christian community has been focused on the Church building and organised around the activities that take place there. Going to that building, and taking part in the activities there, is often understood to be the hallmark of a good Christian.

The Church building is seen as 'sacred space', to which you go to encounter God, leaving outside the world and all its cares.

Have we, the Christian community, chosen to locate God back into our Churches – the new Temple, the new Holy of Holies? Today, as in the time of Jesus, sacred space is safely separated from those who make us uncomfortable, the poor, the unwanted, the despised. Today, as in the time of Jesus, we access God through the priests, not the poor. We have removed God from our streets, our prisons, from our hostels and our drug clinics, from trailers at the side of the road – and we have locked God safely up in our tabernacles. We can, then, oppose the opening of a service for homeless people or drug users on our street, or object to social housing in our neighbourhood, and go to try to find God in our Churches on Sunday.

Mark's Gospel begins with all the people going out to hear the Word of God. Where were they going? They were going to the desert, not to the Temple. They went there to listen to a layman, John the Baptist, not a priest. For Mark, sacred space, where God was to be found, was in the wilderness.

> John the baptiser appeared in the wilderness, proclaiming a baptism of repentance for the forgiveness of sins. And people from the whole Judean countryside and all the people of Jerusalem were going out to him, and were baptised by him in the river Jordan, confessing their sins.
>
> (Mark 1:4-5)

In today's world, some are searching for God but they are not going to the Church. They are bypassing the priests. Many have a strong concern for justice. They are going to South Africa to build houses for the poor; they are going as volunteers to work with Concern, Goal and Trócaire. Many schools have a social immersion programme, where students spend some weeks or months amongst the poor, at home or abroad. This is a life-changing experience for some of them. Maybe they are finding God in the wilderness, where the poor and the outcast live.

5   God is Unfair

For the religious authorities of Jesus' day, God was a God-whose-passion-is-the-observance-of-the-Law. For Jesus, God was a God-whose-passion-is-compassion.

As I said in Chapter 2, for Jewish theology, God's passion was the observance of the Law. In the Law, as revealed in the Hebrew Scriptures, God attempted to show the Jewish people how to relate justly to God and to one another. The Law was an educational tool – it spelt out not only how to worship God but also how to relate to each other without repeating, and therefore re-instating, the oppression in Egypt that they had been liberated from by God. The Law reflected the richness of the relationship between God and the People of God and the authentic values on which that relationship was based. It also reflected the values that underline authentic relationships between people, called every-one to be compassionate and caring to all, and demanded structures that would serve to prevent injustice and oppression amongst the People of God. The Law, therefore, was a rich source of inspiration and instruction for the people.

However, as with every institution, the Jewish world in which Jesus lived was not always faithful to the values it pro-fessed. The Jewish authorities often re-interpreted the Law to suit their own needs and demanded a slavish adherence to the letter of the Law, as interpreted by them, even when this dis-torted authentic relationships with some in their society and caused suffering and pain to others.

Jesus had a great respect for the Law:

> Do not think that I have come to abolish
> the law or the prophets; I have come not
> to abolish but to fulfil. For truly I tell you,
> until heaven and earth pass away, not one
> letter, not one stroke of a letter, will pass
> from the law until all is accomplished.
>   (Matthew 5:17-18)

However, he was very critical of the abuse of the Law and the way in which observance of the Law sometimes caused injustice and suffering to others instead of promoting just and authentic relationships between all.

It is in this context, then, that I describe the God-whose-passion-is-the-observance-of-the-Law as a distortion of the richness of the Law as intended by God. Jesus unequivocally criticises this understanding of God, as it prevents people from reaching a true understanding of God.

The clash between the God-whose-passion-is-the-observance-of-the-Law and the God-whose-passion-is-compassion is far from being just a theological debating issue. It affects our whole way of thinking, acting and behaving towards others.

The God who Judges

The God-whose-passion-is-the-observance-of-the-Law *is a God who judges,* who rewards those who obey and who condemns those who disobey. This is the image of God that many of us have been taught, a God who rewards the good and punishes the wicked.

Believing in a God of the Law, we know exactly where we stand with God. God is entirely predictable. In so far as we do good, obey the Law, we are in God's favour; in so far as we do evil, disobey the Law, we are out of favour with God. Our relationship with God is in *our* hands, within our control, dependent on our behaviour. The God who judges treats us as we deserve. Hence the Pharisees had great difficulty with the way that Jesus treated people.

> Now all the tax collectors and sinners
> were coming near to listen to him. And
> the Pharisees and the scribes were grum-
> bling and saying, 'This fellow welcomes
> sinners and eats with them.' (Luke 15:1-2)

Tax collectors were legalised thieves. They got rich on ripping people off, especially the poor, who were unable to challenge the tax demands that were made on them.

To those who believed in the God-whose-passion-is-the-observance-of-the-Law, it was inconceivable that Jesus would welcome tax collectors in the name of God. It was a source of scandal. God, they believed, would have nothing but condemnation for such rogues. Therefore a truly religious person who sought to do God's will would also, they believed, have nothing but condemnation for them. Jesus' acceptance of the tax collector's invitation to a banquet proved, to some of the Jewish authorities, that Jesus had nothing but contempt for God and for God's Law. Clearly it was God's will, they thought, that he should be got rid of, and as quickly as possible, before he undermined any further people's faith in the true God.

Jesus' treatment of prostitutes no doubt confirmed their opinion.

> One of the Pharisees asked Jesus to eat
> with him, and he went into the Pharisee's
> house and took his place at the table. And
> a woman in the city, who was a sinner,
> having learned that he was eating in the
> Pharisee's house, brought an alabaster
> jar of ointment. She stood behind him at
> his feet, weeping, and began to bathe his
> feet with her tears and to dry them with
> her hair. Then she continued kissing his
> feet and anointing them with the oint-
> ment. Now when the Pharisee who had

invited him saw it, he said to himself, 'If this man were a prophet, he would have known who and what kind of woman this is who is touching him – that she is a sinner.' Jesus spoke up and said to him, 'Simon, I have something to say to you.' 'Teacher,' he replied, 'Speak.' 'A certain creditor had two debtors; one owed five hundred denarii, and the other fifty. When they could not pay, he cancelled the debts for both of them. Now which of them will love him more?' Simon answered, 'I suppose the one for whom he cancelled the greater debt.' And Jesus said to him, 'You have judged rightly.' Then turning toward the woman, he said to Simon, 'Do you see this woman? I entered your house; you gave me no water for my feet, but she has bathed my feet with her tears and dried them with her hair. You gave me no kiss, but from the time I came in she has not stopped kissing my feet. You did not anoint my head with oil, but she has anointed my feet with ointment. Therefore, I tell you, her sins, which were many, have been forgiven; hence she has shown great love. But the one to whom little is forgiven, loves little.'

(Luke 7:36-47)

Not only did Jesus defend the sinner, but he turned the tables on the Pharisee and declared that, by her love, she (who did not obey the Law) was actually closer to God than the one who condemned her (who did obey the Law). Those who were despised and pushed to the margins of society by the just were those who found a welcome from God. The God that Jesus proclaimed, the

God-whose-passion-is-compassion, is entirely unpredictable.

And his treatment of the woman taken in adultery may just have been the last straw for some Pharisees!

> Jesus went to the Mount of Olives. Early in the morning he came again to the temple. All the people came to him and he sat down and began to teach them. The scribes and the Pharisees brought a woman who had been caught in adultery; and making her stand before all of them, they said to him, 'Teacher, this woman was caught in the very act of committing adultery. Now in the law Moses commanded us to stone such women. Now what do you say?' They said this to test him, so that they might have some charge to bring against him. Jesus bent down and wrote with his finger on the ground. When they kept on questioning him, he straightened up and said to them, 'Let anyone among you who is without sin be the first to throw a stone at her.' And once again he bent down and wrote on the ground. When they heard it, they went away, one by one, beginning with the elders; and Jesus was left alone with the woman standing before him. Jesus straightened up and said to her, 'Woman, where are they? Has no one condemned you?' She said, 'No one, sir.' And Jesus said, 'Neither do I condemn you. Go your way, and from now on do not sin again.'
>
> (John 8:1-11)

The Unfair God

The God-whose-passion-is-compassion is totally unfair and most of us actually resent it.

> For the kingdom of heaven is like a land-owner who went out early in the morning to hire labourers for his vineyard. After agreeing with the labourers for the usual daily wage, he sent them into his vineyard. When he went out about nine o'clock, he saw others standing idle in the marketplace; and he said to them, 'You also go into the vineyard, and I will pay you whatever is right.' So they went. When he went out again about noon and about three o'clock, he did the same. And about five o'clock he went out and found others standing around; and he said to them, 'Why are you standing here idle all day?' They said to him, 'Because no one has hired us.' He said to them, 'You also go into the vineyard.'
>
> When evening came, the owner of the vineyard said to his manager, 'Call the labourers and give them their pay, beginning with the last and then going to the first.' When those hired at about five o'clock came, each of them received the usual daily wage. Now when the first came they thought they would receive more; but each of them also received the usual daily wage. And when they received it, they grumbled against the landowner, saying, 'These last worked only one hour, and you have made them equal to us who have borne the burden of the day and the

> scorching heat.' But he replied to one of
> them, 'Friend, I am doing you no wrong;
> did you not agree with me for the usual
> daily wage? Take what belongs to you and
> go; I choose to give to this last the same
> as I give to you. Am I not allowed to do
> what I choose with what belongs to me?
> Or are you envious because I am gener-
> ous?' So the last will be first, and the first
> will be last. (Matthew 20:1-16)

The Trade Unions would have great difficulty with this land-owner! No doubt there would be a picket on the vineyard the following day.

Most of us expect God to be fair, to reward us for the sacrifices and effort that we have made, and to punish those who live selfish and uncaring lives. We want God to be a God of the Law. Like the labourers in the story above, we actually resent a God-whose-passion-is-compassion, for such a God is essentially unfair.

The famous story of the prodigal son is the story of two Gods, a God of the Law and a God of compassion. The younger son, who knows he is a sinner, is entirely dependent on the father being a father of compassion. He returns to throw himself on the father's compassion. If the father were to be predictable, and therefore fair, he ought to punish his younger son for his ingratitude, and reward his elder son for his faithfulness.

The elder brother does not want his father to be *compassion*, he wants him to be *fair*. To his dismay, however, the father is totally unpredictable and treats the sinner even better than he treated the just brother! The just brother resents his father's compassion.

> Then Jesus said, 'There was a man who
> had two sons. The younger of them said
> to his father, "Father, give me the share of
> the property that will belong to me." So
> he divided his property between them.

A few days later the younger son gathered all he had and travelled to a distant country, and there he squandered his property in dissolute living. When he had spent everything, a severe famine took place throughout that country, and he began to be in need. So he went and hired himself out to one of the citizens of that country, who sent him to his fields to feed the pigs. He would gladly have filled himself with the pods that the pigs were eating; and no one gave him anything. But when he came to himself he said, "How many of my father's hired hands have bread enough and to spare, but here I am dying of hunger! I will get up and go to my father, and I will say to him, 'Father, I have sinned against heaven and before you; I am no longer worthy to be called your son; treat me like one of your hired hands.'" So he set off and went to his father. But while he was still far off, his father saw him and was filled with compassion; he ran and put his arms around him and kissed him. Then the son said to him, "Father, I have sinned against heaven and before you; I am no longer worthy to be called your son." But the father said to his slaves, "Quickly, bring out a robe – the best one – and put it on him; put a ring on his finger and sandals on his feet. And get the fatted calf and kill it, and let us eat and celebrate; for this son of mine was dead and is alive again; he was lost and is found!" And they began to celebrate.

'Now his elder son was in the field; and when he came and approached the house, he heard music and dancing. He called one of the slaves and asked what was going on. He replied, "Your brother has come, and your father has killed the fatted calf, because he has got him back safe and sound." Then he became angry and refused to go in. His father came out and began to plead with him. But he answered his father, "Listen! For all these years I have been working like a slave for you, and I have never disobeyed your command; yet you have never given me even a young goat so that I might celebrate with my friends. But when this son of yours came back, who has devoured your property with prostitutes, you killed the fatted calf for him!" Then the father said to him, "Son, you are always with me, and all that is mine is yours. But we had to celebrate and rejoice, because this brother of yours was dead and has come to life; he was lost and has been found."' (Luke 15:11-32)

The elder brother is in all of us who are doing our best to live good lives according to our understanding of the will of God. Compared to those who are leading selfish and self-centred lives, we believe God owes us. If God does not express disapproval of, or condemn in some fashion, those whose lives are sinful, then what is the point in the rest of us trying to live good lives with all the sacrifices and effort that requires? If sinners are going to get the same (or an even better!) welcome from God, why should we bother? So thought the elder brother, and all of us who have the elder brother inside us.

Only sinners can truly welcome a God-whose-passion-is-compassion. The God-whose-passion-is-observance-of-the-Law offers only condemnation to sinners. Sinners cannot rely on their good works to save them, for they have none; they depend on God's compassion. To them, the God that Jesus revealed was, indeed, good news, for it opened the Kingdom of God to them. That Kingdom had been firmly closed to them by the God who rewards the good and punishes the wicked, the God-whose-passion-is-observance-of-the-Law.

Hence, Jesus was welcomed enthusiastically by many who were poor and by many tax collectors and sinners, but rejected by many who were righteous. The God that Jesus revealed was good news to the poor, but bad news for the righteous, who instead of getting some reward from God for their efforts, saw sinners getting the same treatment from God as themselves.

Ireland Today

If we, in Ireland today, wish to follow Jesus, we have to follow the Jesus of 2,000 years ago and not the Jesus of our own wishful imaginations. The followers of Jesus are people-whose-passion-is-compassion. The values, attitudes and behaviour of people-whose-passion-is-compassion are radically transformed by their belief. To believe in a God who reaches out to those whom society disregards or despises compels them to reach out to those on the margins, in support, welcome and acceptance. To believe in a God who forgives the sinner compels them to forgive those who have hurt them, not seven times but seventy times seven times. They are prepared to lay down reputation, riches, property, even life itself, for their brothers and sisters in need.

People-whose-passion-is-compassion seek to build a society whose economic, social and political structures and policies are shaped by a radical concern for those in need, *whether we consider them deserving or not*. To believe in a God who has a passionate concern for those on the margins compels us to struggle to create a society that has a passionate concern for those on the margins. To believe in a God who does not condemn compels us to struggle to create a society that does not condemn.

People-whose-passion-is-compassion are not willing to live quietly, without protest, in a society that is deeply divided. They are not willing to support economic or political policies, even when those policies are beneficial to themselves, if those policies ignore the needs of the poor. They are not willing to support those in society who wish to keep the poor at arm's length.

People-whose-passion-is-compassion are unwilling to restrict their faith to merely individual, personal moral choices. Theirs is a radical faith, which may have to challenge those in power and those who support them at the ballot box.

The resurrection of Jesus was God's confirmation that the God-whose-passion-is-compassion, whom Jesus revealed in his own deeds and words, is, indeed, the true God. Those whose-passion-is-compassion are today the revelation of that God.

6   The New Community of God

When Jesus gathered a community of disciples around him, they asked him to teach them to pray. Jesus gave them a prayer that only the poor could say. How so?

In Jesus' day, the poor had two concerns. The first was getting enough to eat. If they had a little land, life was hard, but they could normally grow enough to feed their family. But more and more were losing their land (through debt incurred to pay the oppressive taxation levied to keep Rome happy, collected by the hated tax collectors, to allow the authorities to live a very comfortable lifestyle, or through outright confiscation by Herod to give to his loyal followers) and entering a more desperate kind of poverty, living on the edge of destitution. They then had to survive from day to day, occasionally getting a day's work that paid enough to feed their family for that day (Matthew 20:1-16). They often went to bed at night not knowing if they would have food the next day.

The second concern, indeed nightmare, for the poor was the possibility of falling into debt. If they had to borrow to feed their family and could not repay, then they, and sometimes their whole family, would be sold into slavery to pay off the debt.

So the prayer that Jesus gave his community to say was the prayer of every poor person in his time:

> Give us this day our daily bread, and forgive us our debts as we forgive those who are indebted to us. (Matthew 6:11-12)

This was not a prayer that the rich could say: their larders were full and there was no question of them ever falling into debt.

It appears that Jesus expected his community of followers to be a community of poor people. Why?

Jesus' Vision Statement

These days, we all have to have vision statements. We set up committees who spend hours and hours deciding where the commas should go! But two thousand years ago, Jesus issued his own vision statement:

> Your Kingdom come ... on earth as it is in
> heaven. (Matthew 6:10)

God had heaven under control, so to speak! The rebellion had been quashed! God now reigned there and God's will is done. Jesus' vision was that the Kingdom of God in heaven, where God's will is always done, would be replicated in the community on earth that Jesus was establishing.

That Kingdom in heaven is a place where everyone is equal, everyone is respected and cared for; where nobody feels rejected, unwanted, marginalised or looked down upon. The community that Jesus was founding, therefore, was a community of equal status, where relationships would be very different to those that people are familiar with. Indeed, those conventional relationships that people took for granted would be turned upside down.

> Whoever wishes to become great among
> you must be your servant. (Mark 10:43)

> Many who are first will be last and the last
> will be first. (Matthew 19:30)

In that community of equality, respect and service of each other, the needs of the poor would be met; the relationships that characterised the community would ensure that the poor would not go hungry and their debts would be forgiven. The prayer of the poor would be heard – *through the community.*

In Jesus, the leader and model of that community, the poor found acceptance, respect and dignity; in the society they were living in, they found only contempt, disdain and rejection. Hence the community that Jesus came to establish appeared extremely attractive to the poor, but very unattractive to those who were better-off and in positions of power and influence, as the status and standing they enjoyed in their society was going to be abolished in this community and their wealth and resources would have to be used to meet the needs of the poor.

THE OLD COMMUNITY OF GOD
In Israel, the community of God, the Covenant, required that debts would be forgiven every seventh year. It was to be a community in which there would be 'no one in need among you' (Deuteronomy 15:4). Poverty and exploitation were to be abolished.

> Every seventh year you shall grant a remission of debts. And this is the manner of the remission: every creditor shall remit the claim that is held against a neighbour, not exacting it of a neighbour who is a member of the community, because the Lord's remission has been proclaimed. Of a foreigner you may exact it, but you must remit your claim on whatever any member of your community owes you. There will, however, be no one in need among you, because the Lord is sure to bless you in the land that the Lord your God is giving you as a possession to occupy. (Deuteronomy 15:1-4)

However, it didn't happen; poverty and exploitation continued.

THE NEW COMMUNITY OF GOD

Jesus was inaugurating the new community of God. In this new community the position of the poor would finally be changed in reality. It was indeed 'good news for the poor'.

> The Spirit of the Lord is upon me, because he has anointed me to bring good news to the poor. (Luke 4:18)
>
> Then he looked up at his disciples and said: 'Blessed are you who are poor, for yours is the kingdom of God. Blessed are you who are hungry now, for you will be filled. Blessed are you who weep now, for you will laugh.' (Luke 6:20-21)

'Those who weep' most likely refers, not to those who are grieving or bereaved, but to those who suffer the daily struggle to survive.

In Matthew's Gospel, the feeding of the multitudes is understood to be a task for the disciples: 'They need not go away; you give them something to eat.' The disciples feed the poor by sharing what resources they have amongst themselves: 'We have nothing here but five loaves and two fish.' And he said, 'Bring them here to me.' In the new community, God transforms what little people have into sufficient for all: 'And all ate and were filled.'

> When he went ashore, he saw a great crowd; and he had compassion for them and cured their sick. When it was evening, the disciples came to him and said, 'This is a deserted place, and the hour is now late; send the crowds away so that they may go into the villages and buy food for themselves.' Jesus said to them,

'They need not go away; you give them something to eat.' They replied, 'We have nothing here but five loaves and two fish.' And he said, 'Bring them here to me.' Then he ordered the crowds to sit down on the grass. Taking the five loaves and the two fish, he looked up to heaven, and blessed and broke the loaves, and gave them to the disciples, and the disciples gave them to the crowds. And all ate and were filled; and they took up what was left over of the broken pieces, twelve baskets full. And those who ate were about five thousand men, besides women and children. (Matthew 14:14-21)

In this community, not only were economic relationships to be transformed within the community, but social and political relationships also.

At that time the disciples came to Jesus and asked, 'Who is the greatest in the kingdom of heaven?' He called a child, whom he put among them, and said, 'Truly I tell you, unless you change and become like children, you will never enter the kingdom of heaven. Whoever becomes humble like this child is the greatest in the kingdom of heaven.'
(Matthew 18:1-5)

Jesus warned them against replicating, within the new community, the relationships of power that existed in the wider society.

But Jesus called them to him and said, 'You know that the rulers of the Gentiles lord it over them, and their great ones are tyrants over them. It will not be so among you; but whoever wishes to be great among you must be our servant, and whoever wishes to be first among you must be your slave; just as the Son of Man came not to be served but to serve and to give his life a ransom for many.'

(Matthew 20:25-28)

In this community, relationships of equality exist.

But you are not to be called rabbi, for you have one teacher, and you are all students. And call no one your father on earth, for you have one Father – the one in heaven. Nor are you to be called instructors, for you have one instructor, the Messiah. The greatest among you will be your servant. All who exalt themselves will be humbled, and all who humble themselves will be exalted.

(Matthew 23:8-12)

The mother of Zebedee who requested that her sons be placed in a position of power in the Kingdom of God failed completely to understand the nature of the Kingdom that Jesus was inaugurating.

Then the mother of the sons of Zebedee came to him with her sons and, kneeling before him, she asked a favour of him. And he said to her, 'What do you want?' She said to him, 'Declare that these two sons of mine will sit, one at your right hand and one at your left, in your kingdom.' But Jesus answered, 'You do not know what you are asking. Are you able to drink the cup that I am about to drink?' They said to him, 'We are able.' He said to them, 'You will indeed drink my cup, but to sit at my right hand and at my left, this is not mine to grant, but it is for those for whom it has been prepared by my Father.'

When the ten heard it, they were angry with the two brothers. But Jesus called them to him and said, 'You know that the rulers of the Gentiles lord it over them, and their great ones are tyrants over them. It will not be so among you; but whoever wishes to be great among you must be your servant, and whoever wishes to be first among you must be your slave; just as the Son of Man came not to be served but to serve, and to give his life a ransom for many.' (Matthew 20:20-28)

This new community was a Kingdom over which God, in the person of Jesus, reigns. It was to be completely different from any other Kingdom.

Then Pilate entered the headquarters again, summoned Jesus, and asked him, 'Are you the King of the Jews?' Jesus answered, 'Do you ask this on your own, or did others tell you about me?' Pilate replied, 'I am not a Jew, am I? Your own nation and the chief priests have handed you over to me. What have you done?' Jesus answered, 'My kingdom is not from this world. If my kingdom were from this world, my followers would be fighting to keep me from being handed over to the Jews. But as it is, my kingdom is not from here.' Pilate asked him, 'So you are a king?' Jesus answered, 'You say that I am a king. For this I was born, and for this I came into the world, to testify to the truth. Everyone who belongs to the truth listens to my voice.' (John 18:33-37)

Jesus' Kingdom is not *from* this world or *of* this world, it is utterly different to any other kingdom in the world. But it was not a spiritual or otherworldly kingdom – it was to be *in* this world, a light for all to see. This community of radically different economic, social and political relationships was to be a model for the world.

> You are the salt of the earth; but if salt has lost its taste, how can its saltiness be restored? It is no longer good for anything, but is thrown out and trampled under foot.
>
> You are the light of the world. A city built on a hill cannot be hid. No one after lighting a lamp puts it under the bushel basket, but on the lamp-stand, and it gives light to all in the house. In the same way, let your light shine before others, so that they may see your good works and give glory to your Father in heaven.
>
> (Matthew 5:13-16)

It had a missionary mandate. It was to become a project of transformation valid for all the nations.

> Go therefore and make disciples of all nations, baptising them in the name of the Father and of the Son and of the Holy

> Spirit, and teaching them to obey every-
> thing that I have commanded you. And
> remember, I am with you always, to the
> end of the age. (Matthew 28:19-20)

This new community, then, represents in history what God desires for all humanity in the face of poverty and oppression – a community that lives together in solidarity and equality, and so in justice and peace, over whom God can reign. The hope and salvation of all humanity are to be found in this community.

This community is the Reign of God in history – God is king of this community and there is no other. God identified himself with Jesus and so God's reign is the Reign of Jesus.

The equality that characterises the Reign of God occurs in the incarnation itself. God came to his people, not by identifying with a religious or priestly leader, not by identifying with some-one with authority but by identifying with a crucified victim of religious and political oppression. This crucified victim, the least in the kingdom of Caesar, is leader and King, the first in the Kingdom of God.

> It will not be so among you; but whoever
> wishes to be great among you must be
> your servant, and whoever wishes to be
> first among you must be your slave; just
> as the Son of Man came not to be served
> but to serve, and to give his life a ransom
> for many.' (Matthew 20:26-28)

The community established by Jesus was to be a community of brothers and sisters, free of all domination. Jesus is Lord and there is no other; Jesus is teacher and there is no other; Jesus is priest, mediator between God and human beings, and there is no other.

Jesus' Mission Statement

Not only do we all now have to have vision statements, but we also have to have mission statements! Even more hours are spent getting this one right. Jesus issued his own mission statement. In the very first words that Jesus uttered as he began his public ministry, he said:

> The Spirit of the Lord has been given to me. He has anointed me to bring the good news to the poor. (Luke 4:18)

That was his mission statement. The good news he came to bring was not something vague, spiritual or other-worldly. It was a visible reality, existing here and now, in the community that Jesus was inaugurating.

> He rolled up the scroll, gave it back to the attendant and sat down. The eyes of all in the synagogue were fixed on him. Then he began to say to them, 'Today this scripture has been fulfilled in your hearing.'
> (Luke 4:20-21)

That community, which was to resemble the Kingdom of God in heaven, was good news to the poor and to those who were willing to live a life of service, in solidarity and equality with the poor. Those who kept themselves apart from the poor would simply not be interested in it. Indeed, they would resent it, as it would not afford them the recognition and status they felt they deserved, and it would make demands on their resources that they might not be willing to accept. Their refusal to live in solidarity with those who were poor would not go unnoticed by God.

> But woe to you who are rich, for you have received your consolation.

Woe to you who are full now, for you will
be hungry.

Woe to you who are laughing now, for
you will mourn and weep.

Woe to you when all speak well of you,
for that is what their ancestors did to the
false prophets. (Luke 6:24-26)

JESUS' TARGET GROUP

Today we not only have to have vision statements and mission
statements, but we have to identify our target group. Jesus too
identified his target group:

Blessed are you who are poor, for yours is
the Kingdom of God. (Luke 6:20)

We find it difficult to accept that Jesus' target group was the poor;
it can make the rest of us, who are not poor, feel excluded and not
appreciated, particularly if we have tried to live good lives and do
our best. But Jesus was not excluding us – he was putting it up
to us!

Now large crowds were travelling with
him; and he turned and said to them,
'Whoever comes to me and does not hate
father and mother, wife and children,
brothers and sisters, yes, and even life
itself, cannot be my disciple. Whoever
does not carry the cross and follow me
cannot be my disciple. For which of you,
intending to build a tower, does not first
sit down and estimate the cost, to see
whether he has enough to complete it?
Otherwise, when he has laid a foundation
and is not able to finish, all who see it will
begin to ridicule him, saying, "This fellow

began to build and was not able to finish." Or what king, going out to wage war against another king, will not sit down first and consider whether he is able with ten thousand to oppose the one who comes against him with twenty thousand? If he cannot, then, while the other is still far away, he sends a delegation and asks for the terms of peace. So therefore, none of you can become my disciple if you do not give up all your possessions.'

(Luke 14:25-33)

The criteria for entering the community that Jesus established was: can you live in radical solidarity with others, in a relationship of equality, respect and dignity with everyone else in this community, including the poor, and thereby ensure that the needs of everyone, including the poor, are met? If so, then you are welcome; if not, you may be a wonderful, hard-working, upright, morally just person – and God will love you for it – but a place in this community is not for you.

Two Rich Men (Luke 18:18; 19:1)

A certain ruler asked him, 'Good Teacher, what must I do to inherit eternal life?' Jesus said to him, 'Why do you call me good? No one is good but God alone. You know the commandments: "You shall not commit adultery; You shall not murder; You shall not steal; You shall not bear false witness; Honour your father and mother."' He replied, 'I have kept all these since my youth.' When Jesus heard this, he said to him, 'There is still one thing lacking. Sell all that you own and distribute the money to the poor, and you will have treasure in heaven; then come, follow me.' But when he heard this, he became sad; for he was very rich. Jesus looked at him and said, 'How hard it is for those who have wealth to enter the kingdom of God! Indeed, it is easier for a camel to go through the eye of a needle than for someone who is rich to enter the kingdom of God.' Those who heard it said, 'Then who can be saved?' He replied, 'What is impossible for mortals is possible for God.'

Here is a man, a very upright man, who has kept all the commandments since his youth, who is keen to do the right thing and approaches Jesus for advice and guidance. This man is every religious vocation director's dream – good living, idealistic, motivated. But Jesus will not accept him into his community of followers!

His unwillingness to use his resources for the benefit of those in the community who are in need makes him a *counter-sign* to the Kingdom of God. Despite his evident goodness, he is not a suitable candidate for the new community that Jesus was inaugurating.

Jesus then meets another rich man, Zacchaeus.

He entered Jericho and was passing through it. A man was there named Zacchaeus; he was a chief tax collector and was rich. He was trying to see who Jesus was, but on account of the crowd he could not, because he was short in stature. So he ran ahead and climbed a sycamore tree to see him, because he was going to pass that way. When Jesus came to the place, he looked up and said to him, 'Zacchaeus, hurry and come down; for I must stay at your house today.' So he hurried down and was happy to welcome him. All who saw it began to grumble and said, 'He has gone to be the guest of one who is a sinner.' Zacchaeus stood there and said to the Lord, 'Look, half of my possessions, Lord, I will give to the poor; and if I have defrauded anyone of anything, I will pay back four times as much.' Then Jesus said to him, 'Today salvation has come to this house, because he too is a son of Abraham. For the Son of Man came to seek out and to save the lost.'

Zacchaeus is invited into the Kingdom ('salvation has come to this house') because, despite his past exploitation of people and a lavish lifestyle funded by that exploitation, he has now found a personal transformation through his encounter with Jesus that has led him to be a witness to that solidarity which is integral to the community of God.

Between the story of the rich man and the story of Zacchaeus, Luke inserts the story of a man who was blind.

As he approached Jericho, a blind man was sitting by the roadside begging. When he heard a crowd going by, he asked what was happening. They told him, 'Jesus of Nazareth is passing by.' Then he shouted, 'Jesus, Son of David, have mercy on me!' Those who were in front sternly ordered him to be quiet; but he shouted even more loudly, 'Son of David, have mercy on me!' Jesus stood still and ordered the man to be brought to him; and when he came near, he asked him, 'What do you want me to do for you?' He said, 'Lord, let me see again.' Jesus said to him, 'Receive your sight; your faith has saved you.' Immediately he regained his sight and followed him, glorifying God; and all the people, when they saw it, praised God.

(Luke 18:35)

This story is, for Luke, the clue that allows us to interpret the stories of the two rich men: the first rich man is blind, unable to see and respond to what God is asking, and his blindness remains uncured; the second rich man is also blind, but in sharing his resources with those in need, his blindness is cured.

The Christian community – both the local Christian communities and the worldwide Christian community – is the community that Jesus founded, intended to be a witness to that community of equality and respect that is the Kingdom of God in heaven. It is for those who wish to affirm, in their own relationships with others, the equality and dignity of everyone, especially the poor, and thereby commit themselves to ensuring that the needs of all, especially the poor, are fulfilled. That is what Jesus did and, therefore, what he calls his followers to do. Jesus intended that the Reign of God would be visible in history in the community of the followers of Jesus. The Christian community must be judged, not by the *quantity* of its membership, but by the *quality* of its witness.

Ireland Today

The Irish people have always been respected for their compassion. Our contributions per capita to international disasters have consistently been amongst the highest in the world. This compassion is no doubt a consequence of the strong Christian faith that Irish people have lived for centuries and brought to other parts of our world.

However, the Gospel describes Jesus' vision for a new community, a vision that calls us to move beyond compassion to solidarity – as Jesus himself did on the Cross.

In compassion, we decide to whom we will reach out and we decide in what way we will reach out. We may decide to support projects for people with disabilities, but not projects for ex-offenders; we may decide to give €100 or we may decide to volunteer one night a week of our time.

Solidarity, however, goes beyond compassion in two ways. First, *we* no longer decide to whom we will reach out. Solidarity is a reaching out to *all* in our world who are victims, who are poor and who are marginalised, whether we like them or not, whether we feel threatened by them or not, whether we judge them to be deserving or not. It is the suffering of others that calls us to solidarity, not the choices that we make.

Second, our response to the suffering of others is chosen not by us, but by those who suffer. Solidarity is a radical commitment to do whatever is required to alleviate their suffering, at whatever cost to ourselves. Thus our *compassion* for those who are homeless may bring us to donate generously to an appeal for funding, which will do a lot of good and alleviate a lot of suffering, but we may at the same time oppose the opening of a hostel for homeless people as being inappropriate for our neighbourhood. Our *solidarity* with those who are homeless, however, may compel us to support such a project, if it is in the interests of homeless people, despite the cost (real or imagined) to ourselves or to our property values. Solidarity compels us to support policies in favour of the poor that may be detrimental to our own interests.

Solidarity, then, is a willingness to respond to the suffering of others with a love that is prepared to see *my* life changed, even radically, in order to bring change to those who suffer. The ultimate expression of solidarity is to be willing to lay down my life in order to bring life to others. It is a recognition that my concern for others is also, ultimately, a concern for myself; that in neglecting others, I am also diminishing myself. As the African proverb says: 'If your neighbour is hungry, your chickens aren't safe.' Solidarity is a recognition that *my* good cannot be achieved independently of *your* good. Solidarity is a commitment to the *common* good in contrast to my own, or any sectoral, good.

The command to 'love one another' calls the Christian community beyond compassion to solidarity. In that solidarity with one another, in that radical sharing, of all that we have and all that we are, with the poor, we find God.

7   Jesus, Liberator – The New Moses

The Reign of God needs a community. That was the function of Israel in the Old Covenant and it is the function of the Christian community in the New Covenant. This community is to be different from all other communities on this earth, not to be isolated from them but to represent for them a new and attractive reality.

> You are the salt of the earth; but if salt has lost its taste, how can its saltiness be restored? It is no longer good for anything, but is thrown out and trampled under foot.
>
> You are the light of the world. A city built on a hill cannot be hid. No one after lighting a lamp puts it under the bushel basket, but on the lamp-stand, and it gives light to all in the house. In the same way, let your light shine before others, so that they may see your good works and give glory to your Father in heaven.
>
> (Matthew 5:13-16)

God had chosen Israel to be the community of God, where God reigns. Through Moses and the Law, God had given instructions as to how this community should live together. Some of these instructions defined the relationships within the community

that would ensure that inequality and injustice would not be perpetuated – they were probably the most radical social legislations
in history:

Every seventh year, the crops were not to be gathered but left
in the fields for the poor to take their fill:

> The Lord spoke to Moses on Mount Sinai,
> saying: 'Speak to the people of Israel and
> say to them: "When you enter the land that
> I am giving you, the land shall observe a
> sabbath for the Lord. Six years you shall
> sow your field, and six years you shall
> prune your vineyard, and gather in their
> yield; but in the seventh year there shall
> be a sabbath of complete rest for the
> land, a sabbath for the Lord: you shall not
> sow your field or prune your vineyard. You
> shall not reap the aftergrowth of your
> harvest or gather the grapes of your
> unpruned vine: it shall be a year of com-
> plete rest for the land. You may eat what
> the land yields during its sabbath – you,
> your male and female slaves, your hired
> and your bound labourers who live with
> you; for your livestock also, and for the
> wild animals in your land all its yield shall
> be for food."' (Leviticus 25:1-8)

Every seventh year, all debts were to be abolished:

> Every seventh year you shall grant a remis-
> sion of debts. And this is the manner of
> the remission: every creditor shall remit
> the claim that is held against a neighbour,
> not exacting it of a neighbour who is a
> member of the community, because the

Lord's remission has been proclaimed. Of a foreigner you may exact it, but you must remit your claim on whatever any member of your community owes you. There will, however, be no one in need among you, because the Lord is sure to bless you in the land that the Lord your God is giving you as a possession to occupy, if only you will obey the Lord your God by diligently observing this entire commandment that I command you today ... If there is among you anyone in need, a member of your community in any of your towns within the land that the Lord your God is giving you, do not be hard-hearted or tight-fisted toward your needy neighbour. You should rather open your hand, willingly lending enough to meet the need, whatever it may be. Be careful that you do not entertain a mean thought, thinking, 'The seventh year, the year of remission, is near,' and therefore view your needy neighbour with hostility and give nothing; your neighbour might cry to the Lord against you, and you would incur guilt. Give liberally and be ungrudging when you do so, for on this account the Lord your God will bless you in all your work and in all that you under-take. Since there will never cease to be some in need on the earth, I therefore command you, 'Open your hand to the poor and needy neighbour in your land.'

(Deuteronomy 15:1-11)

Every seventh year, all slaves were to be freed:

> If a member of your community, whether a Hebrew man or a Hebrew woman, is sold to you and works for you six years, in the seventh year you shall set that person free. And when you send a male slave out from you a free person, you shall not send him out empty-handed. Provide liberally out of your flock, your threshing floor and your wine press, thus giving to him some of the bounty with which the Lord your God has blessed you.
>
> (Deuteronomy 15:12-14)

These laws were meant to ensure that the people of Israel, freed from the oppression of the Pharaoh in Egypt, would not begin to oppress one another. God had rescued them so that the oppression they were experiencing in Egypt would cease. The purpose of these laws was to prevent poverty and indebtedness becoming a permanent feature of people's lives. The people of Israel are the servants of God and cannot become the servants or slaves of any other in Israel.

> Remember that you were a slave in the land of Egypt, and the Lord your God redeemed you; for this reason I lay this command upon you today.
>
> (Deuteronomy 15:15)

> I am the Lord your God, who brought you out of the land of Egypt, to give you the land of Canaan, to be your God.
>
> (Leviticus 25:38)

However, Israel had failed to follow the instructions of God. God's intentions were frustrated by the way in which Israel allowed inequality and injustice to infect the People of God.

The Prophets

The prophets were those who called attention to the infidelity of Israel to the wishes of God.

> Hear, O heavens, and listen, O earth; for the Lord has spoken: I reared children and brought them up, but they have rebelled against me.
>
> The ox knows its owner and the donkey its master's crib; but Israel does not know, my people do not understand.
>
> Ah, sinful nation, people laden with iniquity, offspring who do evil, children who deal corruptly, who have forsaken the Lord, who have despised the Holy One of Israel, who are utterly estranged!
>
> (Isaiah 1:2-4)

Our attempts to win God's favour by offering sacrifice are useless, unless we are doing justice:

> Hear the word of the Lord, you rulers of Sodom! Listen to the teaching of our God, you people of Gomorrah!
>
> 'What to me is the multitude of your sacrifices?' says the Lord; 'I have had enough of burnt offerings of rams and the fat of fed beasts; I do not delight in the blood of bulls, or of lambs, or of goats. When you come to appear before me, who asked this from your hand? Trample my courts no more; bringing offerings is

futile; incense is an abomination to me. New moon and sabbath and calling of convocation – I cannot endure solemn assemblies with iniquity.

Your new moons and your appointed festivals my soul hates; they have become a burden to me, I am weary of bearing them. When you stretch out your hands, I will hide my eyes from you; even though you make many prayers, I will not listen; your hands are full of blood. Wash yourselves; make yourselves clean; remove the evil of your doings from before my eyes; cease to do evil, learn to do good; seek justice, rescue the oppressed, defend the orphan, plead for the widow.'

(Isaiah 1:10-17)

I hate, I despise your festivals, and I take no delight in your solemn assemblies. Even though you offer me your burnt offerings and grain offerings, I will not accept them; and the offerings of well-being of your fatted animals I will not look upon. Take away from me the noise of your songs; I will not listen to the melody of your harps. But let justice roll down like waters, and righteousness like an ever-flowing stream. (Amos 5:21-24)

God is not unaware of the injustice done to his people:

Woe to him who builds his house by unrighteousness, and his upper rooms by injustice; who makes his neighbours work for nothing, and does not give them their wages; who says, 'I will build myself a spacious house with large upper rooms,' and who cuts out windows for it, panelling it with cedar, and painting it with vermilion. Are you a king because you compete in cedar? Did not your father eat and drink and do justice and righteousness? Then it was well with him. He judged the cause of the poor and needy; then it was well. Is not this to know me? says the Lord. But your eyes and heart are only on your dishonest gain, for shedding innocent blood, and for practicing oppression and violence. (Jeremiah 22:13-16)

God is not impressed by our pretence to love and worship God, when, in fact, we are trampling on God's children.

Shout out, do not hold back! Lift up your voice like a trumpet! Announce to my people their rebellion, to the house of Jacob their sins. Yet day after day they seek me and delight to know my ways, as if they were a nation that practiced righteousness and did not forsake the ordinance of their God; they ask of me righteous judgments, they delight to draw near to God.

'Why do we fast, but you do not see? Why humble ourselves, but you do not notice?' Look, you serve your own interest on your fast day, and oppress all your workers. Look, you fast only to quarrel and to fight and to strike with a wicked fist. Such fasting as you do today will not make your voice heard on high. Is such the fast that I choose, a day to humble oneself? Is it to bow down the head like a bullrush, and to lie in sackcloth and ashes? Will you call this a fast, a day acceptable to the Lord? Is not this the fast that I choose: to loose the bonds of injustice, to undo the thongs of the yoke, to let the oppressed go free and to break every yoke? Is it not to share your bread with the hungry and bring the homeless poor into your house; when you see the naked, to cover them and not to hide yourself from your own kin? Then your light shall break forth like the dawn and your healing shall spring up quickly; your vindicator shall go before you, the glory of the Lord shall be your rear guard. Then you shall call and the Lord will answer; you shall cry for help and he will say, 'Here I am.' If you remove the yoke from among you, the pointing of the finger, the speaking of evil, if you offer your food to the hungry and satisfy the needs of the afflicted, then your light shall rise in the darkness and your gloom be like the noonday. The Lord will guide you continually and satisfy your needs in parched places and make your bones strong; and you shall be like a watered garden, like a spring of water, whose waters never fail. (Isaiah 58:1-11)

The prophets not only denounced the infidelity of Israel to God's will, as defined by the Law, but proclaimed God's dream or passion for a new social order, one defined by justice and peace.

The new community of God was to replace the old community of God, which had frustrated God's plans. It was to incorporate God's passion for justice and peace. This community, where God's will would be done, was being inaugurated by Jesus. The old community, which had failed, was being left behind.

> Someone asked him, 'Lord, will only a few be saved?' He said to them, 'Strive to enter through the narrow door; for many, I tell you, will try to enter and will not be able. When once the owner of the house has got up and shut the door, and you begin to stand outside and to knock at the door, saying, 'Lord, open to us,' then in reply he will say to you, 'I do not know where you come from.' Then you will begin to say, 'We ate and drank with you, and you taught in our streets.' But he will say, 'I do not know where you come from; go away from me, all you evildoers!' There will be weeping and gnashing of teeth when you see Abraham and Isaac and Jacob and all the prophets in the kingdom of God, and you yourselves thrown out. Then people will come from east and west, from north and south, and will eat in the kingdom of God. Indeed, some are last who will be first, and some are first who will be last. (Luke 13:23-30)

Jesus, the New Moses

Just as Moses had inaugurated the old community of God, so Jesus is presented in the Gospels as the new Moses inaugurating the new community of God.

Both Moses and Jesus were feared as a threat to the rulers of their time, who sought to eliminate them

a) Pharaoh, fearing that the Israelites, who were slaves in Egypt, might multiply and become a threat to him, ordered that all male children should be put to death. However, Moses escaped by fleeing down the river:

> Then Pharaoh commanded all his people, 'Every boy that is born to the Hebrews you shall throw into the Nile, but you shall let every girl live.'
>
> Now a man from the house of Levi went and married a Levite woman. The woman conceived and bore a son; and when she saw that he was a fine baby, she hid him three months. When she could hide him no longer she got a papyrus basket for him, and plastered it with bitumen and pitch; she put the child in it and placed it among the reeds on the bank of the river. His sister stood at a distance, to see what would happen to him.
>
> The daughter of Pharaoh came down to bathe at the river, while her attendants walked beside the river. She saw the basket among the reeds and sent her maid to bring it. When she opened it, she saw the child. He was crying and she took pity on him, 'This must be one of the Hebrews' children,' she said. Then his sister said to Pharaoh's daughter, 'Shall I go and get you a nurse from the Hebrew women to nurse the child for you?' Pharaoh's daughter said to her, 'Yes.' So the girl went and called the child's mother. Pharaoh's daugh-

ter said to her, 'Take this child and nurse it for me, and I will give you your wages.' So the woman took the child and nursed it. When the child grew up, she brought him to Pharaoh's daughter and she took him as her son. She named him Moses, 'Because,' she said, 'I drew him out of the water.' (Exodus 1:22; 2:10)

b) Herod, hearing that a King had been born that threatened his reign, ordered all male children to be put to death. However, Jesus escaped by fleeing – ironically – into Egypt:

In the time of King Herod, after Jesus was born in Bethlehem of Judea, wise men from the East came to Jerusalem, asking, 'Where is the child who has been born king of the Jews? For we observed his star at its rising and have come to pay him homage.' When King Herod heard this, he was frightened, and all Jerusalem with him; and calling together all the chief priests and scribes of the people, he inquired of them where the Messiah was to be born. They told him, 'In Bethlehem of Judea; for so it has been written by the prophet: "And you, Bethlehem, in the land of Judah, are by no means least among the rulers of Judah; for from you shall come a ruler who is to shepherd my people Israel."'

Then Herod secretly called for the wise men and learned from them the exact time when the star had appeared. Then he sent them to Bethlehem, saying, 'Go and search diligently for the child; and when you have found him, bring me word so that I may also go and pay him homage.' When they had heard the king, they set out; and there, ahead of them, went the star that they had seen at its rising, until it stopped over the place where the child was. When they saw that the star had stopped, they were overwhelmed with joy. On entering the house, they saw the child with Mary his mother; and they knelt down and paid him homage. Then, opening their treasure chests, they offered him gifts of gold, frankincense and myrrh.

And having been warned in a dream not to return to Herod, they left for their own country by another road.

Now after they had left, an angel of the Lord appeared to Joseph in a dream and said, 'Get up, take the child and his mother, and flee to Egypt, and remain there until I tell you; for Herod is about to search for the child, to destroy him.' Then Joseph got up, took the child and his mother by night, and went to Egypt, and remained there until the death of Herod. This was to fulfil what had been spoken by the Lord through the prophet, 'Out of Egypt I have called my son.'

When Herod saw that he had been tricked by the wise men, he was infuriated, and he sent and killed all the children in and around Bethlehem who were two years old or under, according to the time that he had learned from the wise men. Then was fulfilled what had been spoken through the prophet Jeremiah: 'A voice was heard in Ramah, wailing and loud lamentation, Rachel weeping for her children; she refused to be consoled,because they are no more.' (Matthew 2:1)

Both Moses and Jesus went up the mountain and proclaimed God's word to the people

a) Moses went up the mountain to meet God and returned with the Covenant written in stone, to be the 'Constitution' of the People of God:

> Moses brought the people out of the camp to meet God. They took their stand at the foot of the mountain. Now Mount Sinai was wrapped in smoke, because the Lord had descended upon it in fire; the smoke went up like the smoke of a kiln, while the whole mountain shook violently. As the blast of the trumpet grew louder and louder, Moses would speak and God would answer him in thunder. When the Lord descended upon Mount Sinai, to the top of the mountain, the Lord summoned Moses to the top of the mountain, and Moses went up. Then the Lord said to Moses, 'Go down and warn the people not to break through to the Lord to look; otherwise many of them will perish. Even the priests who approach the Lord must consecrate themselves or the Lord will break out against them.' Moses said to the Lord, 'The people are not permitted to come up to Mount Sinai; for you yourself warned us, saying, "Set

limits around the mountain and keep it holy.'" The Lord said to him, 'Go down, and come up bringing Aaron with you; but do not let either the priests or the people break through to come up to the Lord; otherwise he will break out against them.' So Moses went down to the people and told them. (Exodus 19:16-25)
(Moses then gave them the Ten Commandments, the Covenant.)

b) So, too, Jesus goes up the mountain and proclaims the 'constitution' of the new People of God:

When Jesus saw the crowds, he went up the mountain; and after he sat down, his disciples came to him. Then he began to speak, and taught them, saying:
'Blessed are the poor in spirit, for theirs is the kingdom of heaven.
Blessed are those who mourn, for they will be comforted.
Blessed are the meek, for they will inherit the earth.
Blessed are those who hunger and thirst for righteousness, for they will be filled.
Blessed are the merciful, for they will receive mercy.
Blessed are the pure in heart, for they will see God.
Blessed are the peacemakers, for they will be called children of God.
Blessed are those who are persecuted for righteousness' sake, for theirs is the kingdom of heaven.
Blessed are you when people revile you

and persecute you and utter all kinds of evil against you falsely on my account.

Rejoice and be glad, for your reward is great in heaven, for in the same way they persecuted the prophets who were before you.' (Matthew 5:1-12)

The missions of both Moses and Jesus were similar

a) Moses came, sent by God, to liberate the People of God from their oppression in Egypt:

> Then the Lord said, 'I have observed the misery of my people who are in Egypt; I have heard their cry on account of their taskmasters. Indeed, I know their sufferings and I have come down to deliver them from the Egyptians, and to bring them up out of that land to a good and broad land, a land flowing with milk and honey, to the country of the Canaanites, the Hittites, the Amorites, the Perizzites, the Hivites and the Jebusites. The cry of the Israelites has now come to me; I have also seen how the Egyptians oppress them. So come, I will send you to Pharaoh to bring my people, the Israelites, out of Egypt.' (Exodus 3:7-10)

b) So, too, Jesus came, sent by God, to liberate the People of God from their oppression in Israel:

> When he came to Nazareth, where he had been brought up, he went to the synagogue on the sabbath day, as was his custom. He stood up to read, and the

scroll of the prophet Isaiah was given to him. He unrolled the scroll and found the place where it was written: 'The Spirit of the Lord is upon me, because he has anointed me to bring good news to the poor. He has sent me to proclaim release to the captives and recovery of sight to the blind, to let the oppressed go free, to proclaim the year of the Lord's favour.' And he rolled up the scroll, gave it back to the attendant and sat down. The eyes of all in the synagogue were fixed on him. Then he began to say to them, 'Today this scripture has been fulfilled in your hearing.' (Luke 4:16-21)

God, then, had freed the Israelites from their oppressors in Egypt; God had called them to be the People of God and had given them the Laws that would enable them to live in freedom and peace. However, the Israelites failed to observe those laws, and, instead, oppression and injustice were, once again, as in Egypt, the lot of the People of God.

Just as God heard the cries of his people in Egypt and sent Moses to liberate them, God heard the cries of his people in Israel and sent Jesus to liberate them. The old People of God had rejected the Reign of God over them, by the oppression and injustice that they perpetuated; Jesus inaugurates the New People of God, over whom God reigns.

Ireland Today

For many centuries, Irish people were ruled by a foreign nation. The aspiration to be free, to be able to decide our own affairs and shape our own destiny, was always part of our history. Finally, we achieved independence, an independence that we affirmed every chance we got. The Irish language became obligatory in the education of every child, our Catholic heritage was promoted in our ethos and legislation, in order to affirm our separation from our Protestant former colonialists, and we sought to be self-sufficient by developing an agricultural economy. When we joined the EU, we became of age – a nation able to stand alongside other nations, as equals, with our head high. We developed an industrial economy with extraordinary success and became a model for other countries to study and emulate. We were confident enough to be able to acknowledge our inter-dependence on other nations in the global economy. We were able to help other nations with our development aid, given with no strings attached, no self-interest involved, and we were respected as a nation that had lifted itself out of poverty and sought to help other nations to do the same.

However, we need to ask if the ideal of those who struggled and gave their lives for freedom has been realised in our nation. Why do some Irish people today still find themselves rejected and marginalised, left behind and outside, unwanted and unvalued? Have we fulfilled – or abandoned – the commitment given in the Proclamation of Independence that 'The Republic guarantees religious and civil liberty, equal rights and equal opportunities to all its citizens, and declares its resolve to pursue the happiness and prosperity of the whole nation and all of its parts, cherishing all of the children of the nation equally'? Have we exploited economic migrants for our own gain?

That proclamation declared: 'We place the cause of the Irish Republic under the protection of the Most High God.' How would God see us now? Has the oppression and injustice visited upon the people of Ireland by colonial rule been replaced, for some of the people of Ireland, by oppression and injustice visited upon them by their own people?

8   Persecution of the Community

The message of Jesus is personal: it is about our relationship to God. This relationship brings personal transformation in our lives. We live differently because of our relationship to Jesus, who is God.

The message of Jesus cannot remain purely personal; our relationship with Jesus transforms the economic, social and political relationships that exist between those who accept his message and join the community he established. Poverty, exploitation and marginalisation were to be abolished by those new relationships.

It was inevitable that this new community would come into conflict with the world in which it existed, where such poverty, exploitation and marginalisation were deeply ingrained into its very structures. Not only did the existence of this community challenge the conventional modes of thinking and behaving – which in every age is known as 'common sense' – but it also radically challenged those who were living very comfortable lives in that world, those who were wealthy and at the top of the social ladder. It was inevitable therefore that this new community – at every time and in every place – would find itself persecuted.

The Life and Times of Jesus

Jesus did not live and die in cyberspace – he lived and died at a particular point in history. The concrete religious, social, political and cultural situation in which Jesus lived shaped both his own understanding of his mission and the understanding of his followers and of the early Christian communities. Luke emphasises the concrete context of Jesus' life:

> In the fifteenth year of the reign of Emperor Tiberius [AD 29], when Pontius Pilate was governor of Judea, and Herod was ruler of Galilee, and his brother Philip ruler of the region of Ituraea and Trachonitis, and Lysanias ruler of Abilene, during the high priesthood of Annas and Caiaphas. (Luke 3:1-2)

Tiberius had ascended the throne in AD 14 after the death of Caesar Augustus. The Jewish nation had three regions:

- Judea in the south, governed by Pilate with the support of the priests of the Temple in Jerusalem;
- Galilee in the north, governed by Herod;
- to the north and east of Galilee, a district governed by Philip.

Hence, to understand the meaning of Jesus' mission, we have to examine those concrete religious, social, political and cultural contexts in which Jesus lived. We have already looked at some of the religious attitudes and concepts that were dominant at the time of Jesus, as well as the social attitudes and structures that were embedded in the culture of his time – the world of Judaism. Here we look at the political context in which Jesus lived – the Roman Empire – and how he came into conflict with that world.

THE REIGN OF CAESAR
The Reign of God that Jesus came to inaugurate is presented in the Gospels as a potential threat to the other kingdoms that existed at the time of Jesus.

In particular, the Reign of God was contrasted with the reign of Caesar over the Roman Empire. Caesar Augustus, the adopted son of Julius Caesar, was born in 63 BC. In that year, also, Rome conquered Israel. After the assassination of his father, Julius Caesar, in 44 BC, a major civil war erupted in the Roman Empire. It was finally ended with the defeat of Mark Anthony and Cleopatra by Caesar Augustus at the battle of Actium in 31 BC. From then, for the next forty-five years, until AD 14, Caesar Augustus ruled the Roman Empire, which enjoyed an undisturbed peace.

Caesar Augustus was, therefore, considered by the citizens of the Empire as the one who had brought peace on earth. He was revered as a God – throughout the Empire, coins and temples contained inscriptions referring to him as 'Son of God'. (His father, Julius Caesar, had also been revered as a God, believed to be of divine descent, from the God Venus. After his assassination, stories were told of his ascent into heaven to take his place among the gods.) Some inscriptions referred to the contribution that he had made to the world as 'good tidings'.

Titles given to him – 'Son of God', 'Saviour', 'Lord' and 'the one who brought peace to the earth' – were all adopted by Caesar's successors.

The Reign of Jesus

The coming of Jesus to reign over the world was understood by the early Christian communities as a contrast to the reign of the Roman emperors. Jesus, not Caesar, is the Saviour, the Lord, the one who brings peace to the world. Jesus' life and mission are the 'good tidings', not Caesar's life and mission.

> In that region there were shepherds living in the fields, keeping watch over their flock by night. Then an angel of the Lord stood before them, and the glory of the Lord shone around them, and they were terrified. But the angel said to them, 'Do not be afraid; for see – I am bringing you good news [good tidings] of great joy for

all the people: to you is born this day in the city of David a Saviour, who is the Messiah, the Lord. This will be a sign for you: you will find a child wrapped in bands of cloth and lying in a manger.' And suddenly there was with the angel a multitude of the heavenly host, praising God and saying, 'Glory to God in the highest heaven, and on earth peace among those whom he favours!'

(Luke 2:8-14)

The Reign of Jesus was to be very different to the reign of Caesar or any other king. In Israel, the Governor and Royal Court comprised about 7 or 8 per cent of the population and were exceedingly wealthy, while the other 90 per cent or so of the population were poor. Mary's Magnificat affirms that the Reign of Jesus will be very different from that of Caesar –

He has brought down the powerful from their thrones, and lifted up the lowly; he has filled the hungry with good things and sent the rich away empty

– and will be the fulfilment of God's promises to Abraham:

He has helped his servant Israel, in remembrance of his mercy, according to the promise he made to our ancestors, to Abraham and to his descendants forever.

(Luke 1:52-55)

Zechariah refers to the coming of Jesus as mighty Saviour, the one who would save Israel from its enemies, just as Moses once saved Israel from its enemies in Egypt.

> Blessed be the Lord God of Israel, for he has looked favourably on his people and redeemed them. He has raised up a mighty saviour for us in the house of his servant David, as he spoke through the mouth of his holy prophets from of old, that we would be saved from our enemies and from the hand of all who hate us.
>
> (Luke 1:68-71)

Simeon, on meeting Jesus in the Temple, announces Jesus as the salvation of God's people, a light to all other nations that will bring glory to Israel.

> Master, now you are dismissing your servant in peace, according to your word; for my eyes have seen your salvation, which you have prepared in the presence of all peoples, a light for revelation to the Gentiles and for glory to your people Israel. (Luke 2:29-32)

Israel – Yearning for Freedom

Caesar ruled the Jewish land through intermediaries, who had to extract taxes from the people and remit them to Rome. Herod the Great, who ruled in Galilee from 37 BC to 4 BC, was given the title by Caesar of 'King of the Jews' (see John 18:33; 19:22). His rule was brutal, and he hunted down and killed the Jewish resistance movement opposed to Roman rule. He was often referred to by some Jews as Herod the Monstrous. Under Herod, life for the majority of people became very harsh. Increased taxes were levied to pay for Herod's extravagant lifestyle; many landowners had their land confiscated to be given to Herod's favourites and so they were reduced to becoming day labourers or beggars.

When Herod died in 4 BC, riots broke out all over the Jewish land in response to Herod's brutality. Rome sent the army in to quell the riots. The Jewish land was then divided in three parts to be ruled by Herod's three sons – Herod Antipas, Philip and Archelaus. (Two years later, Archelaus was replaced by Pontius Pilate.) Herod Antipas continued his father's brutal rule; it was he who had John the Baptist executed at the whim of the daughter of his wife Herodias and his head handed to her on a plate. In Jerusalem, where Pilate was Governor, the High Priest and the temple authorities were given responsibility for collecting the taxes due to Rome and for maintaining order.

Many of the Jewish citizens were deeply unhappy about this state of affairs. Between the beginning of Rome rule in 63 BC and the great revolt in AD 66, which was suppressed with great brutality including the destruction of the Temple in AD 70, there were many revolutions, all of which were swiftly and brutally repressed by the authorities.

This was the context in which Jesus grew up as a child. Nazareth was a small village, probably with a population of about 200 to 400, about 70 miles north of Jerusalem. However, Nazareth was only 4 miles from a city called Sepphoris, which had been the centre of revolt against Roman rule in 4 BC when Herod the Great died. Sepphoris had been besieged and then invaded by the Roman armies and the revolt quashed with great savagery. However, the memory of what happened in Sepphoris would still be very fresh in the lives of the villagers of Nazareth when Jesus was growing up. Jesus would no doubt have often walked to the newly rebuilt Sepphoris, which, compared to Nazareth, was both very large and very wealthy. He would no doubt have been struck by the enormous disparities between the lives of the citizens of Sepphoris and the poverty of the lives of his own people in Nazareth. He would have heard stories about the harshness of Roman rule, the revolt against Rome and the brutality of Rome's response.

Interestingly, there is no record in the Gospels of Jesus going into the cities to preach, except for Jerusalem. Although the two largest cities, Sepphoris and Tiberias, were close to Nazareth, Jesus appears to have based his preaching in the villages, towns and countryside of Galilee; in other words, his mission was primarily to the Jewish peasant class.

THE PASSOVER FEAST – CELEBRATING FREEDOM

The last week of Jesus' life was spent in Jerusalem. He went up to Jerusalem for the most important feast of the Jewish year, the Passover. During this week, thousands of Jews made the pilgrimage up to the Temple in Jerusalem, the place where God dwelt. It was a dangerous time for the political authorities – the Passover Feast celebrated the liberation of Israel from their foreign oppressors in Egypt; thousands, perhaps hundreds of thousands of Jews were gathering in Jerusalem to celebrate this event. Inevitably among them were some who wished to see the liberation of Israel from their Roman oppressors and were prepared to use violence to achieve it. Hence, during this week, the Romans fortified their garrison in Jerusalem with a large number of soldiers drafted in from outlying barracks.

On the Sunday before the feast – which as Christians we celebrate as Palm Sunday – the Roman Governor, Pontius Pilate, rode into Jerusalem, seated on his magnificent horse, along with a large garrison of cavalry and foot soldiers. People would have come out to witness the pageantry of it: thousands of soldiers with weapons, gold eagles mounted on poles, the beating of drums. This procession of the Roman Governor and his soldiers was not just the symbol of a political system that created and maintained poverty, enormous inequality and oppression but it was the very means by which this system maintained itself.

On Palm Sunday, Jesus also entered Jerusalem, from the other side of the city, seated on a donkey. This was not a coincidence; this procession was planned in advance and carefully thought out:

> When they had come near Jerusalem and had reached Bethphage, at the Mount of Olives, Jesus sent two disciples, saying to them, 'Go into the village ahead of

you, and immediately you will find a donkey tied, and a colt with her; untie them and bring them to me. If anyone says anything to you, just say this, "The Lord needs them." And he will send them immediately.'

This took place to fulfil what had been spoken through the prophet, saying, 'Tell the daughter of Zion, Look, your king is coming to you, humble, and mounted on a donkey, and on a colt, the foal of a donkey.' The disciples went and did as Jesus had directed them; they brought the donkey and the colt, and put their cloaks on them, and he sat on them. A very large crowd spread their cloaks on the road, and others cut branches from the trees and spread them on the road. The crowds that went ahead of him and that followed were shouting, 'Hosanna to the Son of David! Blessed is the one who comes in the name of the Lord! Hosanna in the highest heaven!' When he entered Jerusalem, the whole city was in turmoil, asking, 'Who is this?' The crowds were saying, 'This is the prophet Jesus from Nazareth in Galilee.' (Matthew 21:1-11)

This was a deliberate prophetic act on Jesus' part, intended to contrast with the procession of Pontius Pilate. Matthew tells us the meaning of Jesus' entry into Jerusalem in this way:

This took place to fulfil what had been spoken through the prophet, saying, 'Tell the daughter of Zion, look, your king is coming to you, humble, and mounted on a donkey, and on a colt, the foal of a donkey.' (Matthew 21:4-5)

The full text of the prophet that Matthew quotes is:

> Rejoice greatly, O daughter Zion! Shout aloud, O daughter Jerusalem! Lo, your king comes to you; triumphant and victorious is he, humble and riding on a donkey, on a colt, the foal of a donkey. He will cut off the chariot from Ephraim and the war horse from Jerusalem; and the battle bow shall be cut off, and he shall command peace to the nations; his dominion shall be from sea to sea, and from the River to the ends of the earth. (Zechariah 9:9-10)

The Reign of Jesus was to be a reign of peace that would banish chariots, war horses and battle bows; this reign would be from sea to sea, to the ends of the earth. It would abolish the reign of Caesar and every other reign where injustice, oppression and war existed. Jesus intended his procession – which today we would call a 'counter-demonstration' – to contrast the two reigns, the Reign of God and the reign of Caesar, two very different visions of life on earth.

JESUS AND THE AUTHORITIES
Jesus made no secret of his opposition to the authorities in Jerusalem. Mark describes Jesus, in this final week of his life, walking in the Temple when the chief priests, the scribes and the elders came up to him.

> Then he began to speak to them [the chief priests, scribes and elders] in parables. 'A man planted a vineyard, put a fence around it, dug a pit for the wine press

and built a watchtower; then he leased it to tenants and went to another country. When the season came, he sent a slave to the tenants to collect from them his share of the produce of the vineyard. But they seized him and beat him, and sent him away empty-handed. And again he sent another slave to them; this one they beat over the head and insulted. Then he sent another, and that one they killed. And so it was with many others; some they beat and others they killed. He had still one other, a beloved son. Finally he sent him to them, saying, "They will respect my son." But those tenants said to one another, "This is the heir; come, let us kill him, and the inheritance will be ours." So they seized him, killed him and threw him out of the vineyard. What then will the owner of the vineyard do? He will come and destroy the tenants and give the vineyard to others. Have you not read this scripture: "The stone that the builders rejected has become the cornerstone; this was the Lord's doing, and it is amazing in our eyes"?' When they realised that he had told this parable against them, they wanted to arrest him, but they feared the crowd. So they left him and went away.

(Mark 12:1-12)

The chief priests, the scribes and the elders (the political/religious leaders of Jerusalem) were in no doubt that Jesus was talking about them. They had failed to be good stewards of God's kingdom (the vineyard) and the kingdom was to be given to others (the disciples of Jesus).

Jesus is openly critical of the social and political system, presided over by the Pharisees, scribes and lawyers, in which he lived.

> As he taught, he said, 'Beware of the scribes, who like to walk around in long robes, and to be greeted with respect in the marketplaces, and to have the best seats in the synagogues and places of honour at banquets! They devour widows' houses and for the sake of appearance say long prayers. They will receive the greater condemnation.' He sat down opposite the treasury and watched the crowd putting money into the treasury. Many rich people put in large sums. A poor widow came and put in two small copper coins, which are worth a penny. Then he called his disciples and said to them, 'Truly I tell you, this poor widow has put in more than all those who are contributing to the treasury. For all of them have contributed out of their abundance; but she out of her poverty has put in everything she had, all she had to live on.' (Mark 12:38-44)

Clearly, Mark links Jesus' criticism of the scribes 'who devour widow's houses' with the poor widow who puts in all she has. Instead of taking the widow's few mites, the scribes should have been supporting her! Perhaps Mark had in mind Isaiah's criticism of the rulers of his own time:

> Ah, you who make iniquitous decrees, who write oppressive statutes, to turn aside the needy from justice and to rob

the poor of my people of their right, that widows may be your spoil and that you may make the orphans your prey! What will you do on the day of punishment, in the calamity that will come from far away? To whom will you flee for help, and where will you leave your wealth? (Isaiah 10:1-3)

Jesus indicts the leaders of his people:

'But woe to you, scribes and Pharisees, hypocrites! For you lock people out of the kingdom of heaven. For you do not go in yourselves, and when others are going in, you stop them.

'Woe to you, scribes and Pharisees, hypocrites! For you cross sea and land to make a single convert, and you make the new convert twice as much a child of hell as yourselves.

'Woe to you, blind guides, who say, "Whoever swears by the sanctuary is bound by nothing, but whoever swears by the gold of the sanctuary is bound by the oath." You blind fools! For which is greater, the gold or the sanctuary that has made the gold sacred? And you say, "Whoever swears by the altar is bound by nothing, but whoever swears by the gift that is on the altar is bound by the oath." How blind you are! For which is greater, the gift or the altar that makes the gift sacred?

'Woe to you, scribes and Pharisees, hypocrites! For you tithe mint, dill and cumin, and have neglected the weightier matters of the law: justice and mercy and faith. It is these you ought to have practiced without neglecting the others. You blind guides! You strain out a gnat but swallow a camel!

'Woe to you, scribes and Pharisees, hypocrites! For you clean the outside of the cup and of the plate, but inside they are full of greed and self-indulgence. You blind Pharisee! First clean the inside of the cup, so that the outside also may become clean.

'Woe to you, scribes and Pharisees, hypocrites! For you are like whitewashed tombs, which on the outside look beautiful, but inside they are full of the bones of the dead and of all kinds of filth. So you also on the outside look righteous to others, but inside you are full of hypocrisy and lawlessness.

'Woe to you, scribes and Pharisees, hypocrites! For you build the tombs of the prophets and decorate the graves of the righteous, and you say, "If we had lived in the days of our ancestors, we would not have taken part with them in shedding the blood of the prophets." Thus you testify against yourselves that you are descendants of those who murdered the prophets. Fill up, then, the measure of your ancestors. You snakes, you brood of vipers! How can you escape being sentenced to hell? Therefore I send you prophets, sages and scribes, some of whom you will kill and crucify, and some you will flog in your synagogues and pur-

sue from town to town, so that upon you
may come all the righteous blood shed
on earth, from the blood of righteous
Abel to the blood of Zechariah son of
Barachiah, whom you murdered between
the sanctuary and the altar. Truly I tell you,
all this will come upon this generation.'
(Matthew 23:1-36)

These are not the words of someone who came only to lead us as
individuals into a new personal relationship with God. These are
the words of someone who is appalled at the way in which the
people were being ruled, at the hypocrisy of the rulers, their
oppression of the people and his passionate desire that things
would change, indeed be reversed. The Kingdom of God was the
centre of Jesus' mission – the kingdom of Caesar in which he is
living is far from the Kingdom of God. Jesus came to inaugurate
the Kingdom of God:

Now after John was arrested, Jesus came
to Galilee, proclaiming the good news of
God, and saying, 'The time is fulfilled,
and the kingdom of God has come near;
repent and believe in the good news.'
(Mark 1:15)

Jesus was persecuted and executed for preaching his vision for
the Kingdom of God:

Then the chief priests and the elders of
the people gathered in the palace of the
high priest, who was called Caiphas, and
they conspired to arrest Jesus by stealth
and kill him. But they said, 'Not during
the festival, or there may be a riot among
the people.' (Matthew 26:3-5)

CRUCIFIXION

Jesus was not just put to death, he was crucified. The Jewish authorities, if they had the power to put a person to death, would have condemned them to death by stoning. The Roman authorities had various other modes of capital punishment, such as beheading. Crucifixion was the capital punishment reserved for rebellious slaves and those who sought to overthrow the Roman rule. Crucifixion was always a very violent and public punishment intended as a deterrent to others who might be tempted to rebel. Crucifixion was the penalty imposed by the Romans on those who refused to accept established authority.

Clearly the early Christian Church understood that the religious authorities handed Jesus over to the Roman Governor alleging that he was a King and that his Kingdom was a threat to the Roman rule. The political authorities convicted him on this basis and crucified him.

> Pilate tried to release him, but the Jews cried out, 'If you release this man, you are no friend of the emperor. Everyone who claims to be a king sets himself against the emperor.' When Pilate heard these words, he brought Jesus outside and sat on the judge's bench at a place called The Stone Pavement, or in Hebrew Gabbatha. Now it was the day of Preparation for the Passover; and it was about noon. He said to the Jews, 'Here is your King!' They cried out, 'Away with him! Away with him! Crucify him!' Pilate asked them, 'Shall I crucify your King?' The chief priests answered, 'We have no king but the emperor.' Then he handed him over to them to be crucified.
>
> So they took Jesus; and carrying the cross by himself, he went out to what is

called The Place of the Skull, which in
Hebrew is called Golgotha. There they
crucified him, and with him two others,
one on either side, with Jesus between
them. Pilate also had an inscription written and put on the cross. It read, 'Jesus of
Nazareth, the King of the Jews.' Many of
the Jews read this inscription, because
the place where Jesus was crucified was
near the city; and it was written in
Hebrew, in Latin, and in Greek. Then the
chief priests of the Jews said to Pilate, 'Do
not write, "The King of the Jews", but,
"This man said, I am King of the Jews".'
Pilate answered, 'What I have written I
have written.' (John 19:12-22)

The soldiers who crucified him understood that he was being
crucified because of his claim to Kingship.

Then Pilate took Jesus and had him
flogged. And the soldiers wove a crown of
thorns and put it on his head, and they
dressed him in a purple robe. They kept
coming up to him, saying, 'Hail, King of
the Jews!' and striking him on the face.
(John 19:1-3)

Jesus' passion for a new world in which personal transformation
would translate into new ways of relating to each other and new
forms of leadership was understood, both by the Jewish authorities and by Jesus' own disciples, as a challenge to the existing
social and political structures. Jesus' execution was inevitable; he
did not need to be a prophet to foresee what was going to happen
to him. His message was good news to the poor, that their
poverty and oppression would be overcome in the new commu-

nity of followers he was inaugurating; he brought his message to Jerusalem, the centre of Jewish faith, at the feast of the Passover, a time when thousands of people would be present on pilgrimage, and there challenged the authorities very publicly.

It was Jesus' passion for the Kingdom of God, a Kingdom here on earth of justice, equality and peace, that led to his passion on the cross.

During his time on earth, he sent out his followers to preach his vision for the Kingdom of God.

> These twelve Jesus sent out with the following instructions: 'Go nowhere among the Gentiles, and enter no town of the Samaritans, but go rather to the lost sheep of the house of Israel. As you go, proclaim the good news, 'The kingdom of heaven has come near.' Cure the sick, raise the dead, cleanse the lepers, cast out demons. You received without payment; give without payment. (Matthew 10:5-8)

After the Resurrection, the Christian community understands that, just as Jesus came so that 'God's Kingdom might come on earth, as it is in heaven', so now that he has risen, he has been given by God 'all authority in heaven and earth', thus abolishing all other authority in heaven or earth, and has sent out his disciples to bring in all nations to the community of which Jesus is Lord.

> And Jesus came and said to them, 'All authority in heaven and on earth has been given to me. Go therefore and make disciples of all nations.' (Matthew 28:18-19)

The followers of Jesus, who proclaim that Jesus is King and there is no other, and who seek to create a community that defies the conventional economic, social and political relationships that are characteristic of society as we know it, can only expect the same treatment as their Master.

> If the world hates you, be aware that it hated me before it hated you. If you belonged to the world, the world would love you as its own. Because you do not belong to the world, but I have chosen you out of the world – therefore the world hates you. Remember the word that I said to you, 'Servants are not greater than their master.' If they persecuted me, they will persecute you; if they kept my word, they will keep yours also. But they will do all these things to you on account of my name, because they do not know him who sent me. (John 15:18-21)

Ireland Today

The passion of Christians for a new world, a world in which the dignity and humanity of each human being is respected, requires a revolution in the economic, social and political relationships that are currently characteristic of our societies and of our globalised capitalist structures. To challenge those structures, by our words and by our actions, is to invite the criticism, hostility and opposition of many in those societies.

Two hundred and twenty thousand houses and apartments in Ireland are lying permanently empty, while five thousand people are homeless – that is what happens in a system where housing becomes a commodity to be bought and sold, like stocks and shares, instead of a basic need of every citizen. In Africa, shopping malls with every conceivable luxury good are available to those who can afford them, while people die from hunger and disease a mile away. Drugs are not available to the poor in many parts of our world because patent rights, which preserve the profits of drug companies, take precedence over the health and lives of the poor. Obscene poverty exists side by side with obscene wealth; exploitation and marginalisation are seen as inevitable, if unfortunate, byproducts of a world where everything carries a price, where 'profit [is] the key motive for economic progress, competition the supreme law of economics, and private ownership of the means of production an absolute right that has no limits and carries no corresponding social obligation' (*On the Development of Peoples*, Pope Paul vi, 1967, para 26).

Increasingly, in Ireland, everything, including our basic needs, has become a commodity to be purchased by those who can afford to purchase it: housing, education, health, childcare, care of the elderly, development and education of children with special needs, are all readily available if you have the resources to obtain them. If not, you are dependent on the willingness of society to make available resources that may be inadequate for the proper development and care that human dignity requires. The basic needs of each individual are human rights to which each person ought to be entitled as a matter of course and should not be dependent on the goodwill – or otherwise – of others.

All injustice is a denial of the dignity of the person. Homeless people in Ireland live with the knowledge that they are just not important enough for this society to ensure they have a place that they can call home – although houses lie vacant. Those who are hungry in Southern Africa know that they are just not important enough for our world to bother trying to get food to them – although food is available. Those who lack essential medicines know that they are of less importance than the profits of pharmaceutical companies.

To challenge injustice, in the name of the dignity of every human being, is to risk ridicule, opposition and rejection from many in society who do not wish the structures, policies or financial resource allocations to change. To challenge the structures, policies or resource allocations that benefit the comfortable is to risk the wrath of those who have too much to lose.

To live the Gospel of solidarity, to be driven by the passion of

Jesus for an end to poverty and exploitation and the building of a world of justice and peace that reflects the vision of God is not for those who want a quiet life.

9 Forgiveness within the Community

All communities celebrate special moments in the life of that community. They have celebrations when new members join the community; they celebrate events that they consider significant for the community; they celebrate the appointment or election of leaders to the community.

The Christian community is no different: it, too, is a community of people who live their lives together and who celebrate those moments of special importance in the life of their community.

The primary significance of all the sacraments lies in community:

- Sacrament of Baptism is the celebration of the community at the entry into their midst of a new member;
- Sacrament of Confirmation is the celebration of the community at one of their children reaching adulthood;
- Sacrament of Marriage is the celebration of the community at the commitment in love of one (or both) of their members to each other;
- Sacrament of the Sick is the prayer of the community for healing or a happy death of one of their community;
- Sacrament of Holy Orders is the anointing of one of the community to be a leader of that community;
- Sacrament of the Eucharist is the celebration of the community of the death and resurrection of Jesus that brought them

together; and their commitment to love one another as Jesus loved them;

- Sacrament of Penance is the request to the community for forgiveness from someone who has offended another within the community.

If there is no community, then the primary significance of the sacraments is lost; we have to find, indeed invent, an alternative significance. Today, with the weakening of the bonds within community, or sometimes the almost total breakdown or absence of community, the sacraments have come to be understood primarily as channels of grace to *individuals*. Undoubtedly they are, but this is not the primary significance of the sacraments. In the absence of community, the sacraments have become, for many Christians, social occasions, events dictated by social convention, rituals to be undergone, frequently boring and irrelevant to their 'real' lives. The Eucharist may become 'a Sunday duty'; the 'sign of peace', where we reach out to our neighbour, an unwelcome intrusion into one's personal time with God.

In particular, many Christians now find the sacrament of confession totally unnecessary and irrelevant in its present form. While the community aspect of confession is not totally absent (the priest is understood to represent the community), it is largely theoretical and unreal for most people.

In the new community of Jesus, the sacraments marked significant moments in the lives of the members of that community, moments that the community together celebrated. Among those moments were the reconciliation of differences between members of the community, differences caused by the weakness or sinfulness of its members. Such reconciliation was an integral part of life in the community, as without a genuine reconciliation, the community would fall apart.

Hence in the Gospels, Jesus emphasises, again and again, the need for forgiveness within the community.

Then Peter came and said to him, 'Lord, if another member of the church sins against me, how often should I forgive? As many as seven times?' Jesus said to him, 'Not seven times, but, I tell you, seventy-seven times.

For this reason the kingdom of heaven may be compared to a king who wished to settle accounts with his slaves. When he began the reckoning, one who owed him ten thousand talents was brought to him; and, as he could not pay, his lord ordered him to be sold, together with his wife and children and all his possessions, and payment to be made. So the slave fell on his knees before him, saying, "Have patience with me, and I will pay you everything." And out of pity for him, the lord of that slave released him and forgave him the debt. But that same slave, as he went out, came upon one of his fellow slaves who owed him a hundred denarii; and seizing him by the throat, he said, "Pay what you owe." Then his fellow slave fell down and pleaded with him, "Have patience with me, and I will pay you." But he refused; then he went and threw him into prison until he would pay the debt. When his fellow slaves saw what had happened, they were greatly distressed, and they went and reported to their lord all that had taken place. Then his lord summoned him and said to him, "You wicked slave! I forgave you all that debt because you pleaded with me. Should you not have had mercy on your fellow slave, as I had mercy on you?" And in anger his lord handed him over to be tortured until he would pay his entire debt.

So my heavenly Father will also do to every one of you, if you do not forgive your brother or sister from your heart.'

(Matthew 18:21-35)

Seven was the number that signified perfection. Hence Peter's question was, 'Must my forgiveness be perfect?' Jesus replies, 'Not only perfect, but way, way beyond perfect.'

Forgiveness – The Image of God's Forgiveness

Forgiving each other within the community was modelled on the forgiveness of each member by God. If God has forgiven us, then we too must forgive one another. If we are to forgive one another in a way that goes 'beyond perfection', then it is because God has forgiven us in the same way.

As I said in Chapter 4, we can never understand God. When we talk about God's forgiveness, we use a concept, 'forgiveness', which comes from our experience of people forgiving one another, sometimes in a heroic and extraordinary way. But God's forgiveness goes infinitely beyond this human concept of forgiveness.

In the story above from Matthew's Gospel, the servant refused to forgive his fellow servant a debt of one hundred denarii. A denarius was the equivalent of a day's pay for a manual labourer. A hundred denarii, for such a person, was a not insignificant sum, the equivalent of three months' wages.

But the Master had forgiven the servant a debt of ten thousand talents. One talent was worth six thousand denarii. Ten thousand talents was worth sixty million denarii, the equivalent of more than 150, 000 years' wages! Jesus uses this hugely exaggerated sum to illustrate how great is God's forgiveness; God's forgiveness is infinite, it is greater than any sin we can commit, and so, in response to being forgiven so much, we ought in turn forgive one another.

One of the questions I am frequently asked by young homeless people is 'You won't give up on me, will you?' They ask this question usually when things are going wrong for them; perhaps they have gone back to using drugs or they have done something of which they know I will strongly disapprove. They may feel that they have let me down and wonder will I be angry with them to the point of rejecting them. Their question is: do I care for them only when they are doing well, when their behaviour is living up to my expectations of them, or do I care for them because of who they are? Their fear is that because they are now behaving in a way that they expect me to disapprove of, my care and concern for them will evaporate. This may well have been their experience to date.

This is actually a very fundamental question; indeed, it relates to our understanding of God. Their question is: do I care for them *unconditionally*? Because if I show – as they expect me to – that I care for them only because of their (good) behaviour, then they themselves *as persons* are of little value to me. Their value then depends on their behaviour. In this question, their very dignity as persons is at stake.

God loves us unconditionally. God's love does not depend on our behaviour. But forgiveness is the greatest form of love; to forgive someone who has offended against us is the greatest expression of our love for them. God forgives us unconditionally. God's forgiveness does not depend on our behaviour. God's love is so perfect that God forgives us even before we repent. Conventional thinking believes that we must repent first, then subsequently God forgives us. But perhaps repentance comes from the experience of being forgiven unconditionally; the infinite love of God for us, expressed in that unconditional forgiveness, draws us to repentance, to expressing our sorrow at having offended the One who has loved us so much. God does not punish us or threaten to punish us; when we break our relationship with God through sin, God restores that relationship, not by punishing us, not by getting his own back on us, not by teaching us a lesson – but by forgiving us, freely and unconditionally.

Some will argue that, if we remove the threat of punishment, people will feel free to do whatever they want. We need a God who will punish wrong-doers. But this is to use God to control people's behaviour. God cannot be used. The God that Jesus revealed was not a God of the Law, who punishes the wicked and rewards the good. God rather seeks out the sinner before the sinner seeks out God.

> Now all the tax collectors and sinners were coming near to listen to him. And the Pharisees and the scribes were grumbling and saying, 'This fellow welcomes sinners and eats with them.' So he told them this parable: 'Which one of you, having a hundred sheep and losing one of them, does not leave the ninety-nine in the wilderness and go after the one that is lost until he finds it? When he has found it, he lays it on his shoulders and rejoices. And when he comes home, he calls together his friends and neighbours, saying to them, "Rejoice with me, for I have found my sheep that was lost." Just so, I tell you, there will be more joy in heaven over one sinner who repents than over ninety-nine righteous persons who need no repentance.' (Luke 15:1-7)

Love as Forgiveness

If a community lives in love, forgiveness is the greatest expression of that love. No human community can survive without a strong willingness to forgive the sin and human weakness that are part of being human. The community founded by Jesus had only one rule: 'Love one another as I have loved you.' As God's love and forgiveness is unconditional, so the love and forgiveness of the members of the community of Jesus was to be unconditional.

Forgiveness is the highest expression of love; to forgive someone, particularly if that person has not expressed any repentance, is the greatest love one person can show for another. God's love is infinite; and the ultimate expression of that love is God's forgiveness.

Ireland Today

Many people have been inspired by the example of some in Northern Ireland who have lost loved ones to gun or bomb. Despite the suffering that has been imposed on them, they are able to say, publicly, that they forgive those who have caused them such suffering. The evil that has been done to them is overcome, not by vengeance or revenge, but by forgiveness. Gordon Wilson, who lost a daughter in the Enniskillen bombings in 1987, is one such saint. Shortly after the murder of his daughter he was able to go on television and state that he had forgiven those who had committed this atrocity against him. Forgiveness of those who have hurt them does not bring their loved ones back, nor take away the pain of loss – nothing, not even vengeance, can do that. For them, justice is fulfilled in forgiveness. If they, whom God created, can find the fulfilment of justice in forgiveness, then surely the God who created them also finds the fulfilment of God's justice in forgiveness. Forgiveness is the soul of justice.

Today in Ireland most people have been the victims of crime at some point in their lives. Sometimes the crimes committed against them, or some of their family, have had a devastating effect on their lives and their health. Those who have committed the crimes may never express any remorse. How can one expect such people to be able to find forgiveness in their heart?

Those who have been the victims of crime need, above all, the support of the community. The compassion and care of the community, their supportive presence and their expressions of love, and of indignation at the unnecessary suffering which has been inflicted on the victim, can bring some comfort to them in their pain. Such support may be necessary for a very long time, especially where the person was particularly traumatised by the experience.

However, full healing requires the strength to find forgiveness. Anger, bitterness and resentment, understandable as it is, destroy one's spirit just as much, or more, than the suffering that another person has inflicted. A person cannot regain the joy and peace, which is the hallmark of the person who knows that they are loved by God, until they have found it in them to forgive. Those who can find it in them to forgive are the living saints in our midst.

A mother came to see me to ask my advice. 'Father, my son is a drug user, I don't know what to do. He has robbed everything in the house; sometimes he would come home looking for money for drugs, and when I didn't have it to give him, he would smash all the windows in the house; sometimes he has even hit me when I wasn't able to give him money. What am I going to do?' 'And where is he now,' I asked. 'He's in jail, Father, it's the first peace I have had in five years.' 'Do you go to visit him?' I asked. 'Ah, Father, every Saturday without fail, I go up to see him. Sure isn't he still my son.'

10   Reflections on a Spirituality for the New Community

The spirituality of the Christian, within the Christian community, is one of 'letting go': letting go of possessions, letting go of status, letting go of power and above all letting go of our securities. All our lives are a 'letting go'. The Gospels remind us that everything we have, everything we possess, is a gift to us from God. Our life itself, our health, our education, our family, our friends, our property, our assets, our jobs, everything is a gift given freely to us – but only given on loan. All the gifts we have been given have to be given back to God. As we grow older, we have to give back to God our parents, our health, our jobs until that final moment when we give back all that remains, life itself, along with our property, our assets and our wealth. 'Letting go' is the spirituality that conforms to the essence of our existence as human beings, destined to grow old and die. Life is a giving back to God what God has already given to us. It is in letting go, not in accumulating or holding on to, that we find our true happiness and our fulfilment.

> Someone in the crowd said to him, 'Teacher, tell my brother to divide the family inheritance with me.' But he said to him, 'Friend, who set me to be a judge or arbitrator over you?' And he said to them, 'Take care! Be on your guard against

all kinds of greed; for one's life does not consist in the abundance of possessions.' Then he told them a parable: 'The land of a rich man produced abundantly. And he thought to himself, "What should I do, for I have no place to store my crops?" Then he said, "I will do this: I will pull down my barns and build larger ones, and there I will store all my grain and my goods. And I will say to my soul, 'Soul, you have ample goods laid up for many years; relax, eat, drink, be merry.'" But God said to him, "You fool! This very night your life is being demanded of you. And the things you have prepared, whose will they be?" So it is with those who store up treasures for themselves but are not rich toward God.' (Luke 12:13-21)

Letting Go of our Securities

The 'letting go' described in the Gospels is above all a letting go of our false securities. If life is a constant letting go of the gifts that God has given to us, it is also a letting go of the securities those gifts bring: the moment we are born, we let go of the security of our mother's womb; at six years of age, we happily walk down the street with our hand in our mother's hand; at sixteen years of age, we wouldn't be seen dead walking down the street holding hands with our mother! As we get older, we leave the security of our family home and move into our own accommodation (if we can get it!); we leave the security of family and create a new family for ourselves; and finally, we let go of the last security of all, our life. Letting go of all the securities in our lives allows us to place our security in God alone.

He said to his disciples, 'Therefore I tell you, do not worry about your life, what you will eat, or about your body, what you will wear. For life is more than food, and the body more than clothing. Consider the ravens: they neither sow nor reap, they have neither storehouse nor barn, and yet God feeds them. Of how much more value are you than the birds! And can any of you by worrying add a single hour to your span of life? If then you are not able to do so small a thing as that, why do you worry about the rest? Consider the lilies, how they grow: they neither toil nor spin; yet I tell you, even Solomon in all his glory was not clothed like one of these. But if God so clothes the grass of the field, which is alive today and tomorrow is thrown into the oven, how much more will he clothe you – you of little faith!

And do not keep striving for what you are to eat and what you are to drink, and do not keep worrying. For it is the nations of the world that strive after all these things, and your Father knows that you need them. Instead, strive for his king-dom, and these things will be given to you as well. Do not be afraid, little flock, for it is your Father's good pleasure to give you the kingdom. Sell your possessions and give alms. Make purses for yourselves that do not wear out, an unfailing treas-ure in heaven, where no thief comes near and no moth destroys. For where your treasure is, there your heart will be also.'

(Luke 12:22-34)

The Values of a Consumer Economy

A spirituality of 'letting go' is counter-cultural. The values in a spirituality of 'letting go' are in direct contradiction to the values of our consumer, capitalist economy.

Fulfilment as Consumption

The Western capitalist economy in which we are so successfully embedded feeds on consumerism. Consumerism is the food that enables it to grow. It must persuade us to purchase much and often. If it fails to do so, economic growth would falter and ultimately collapse.

To persuade us to purchase much and often, it must seek to convince us that *it is in consuming that our needs can be fulfilled;* our fulfilment and our happiness is to be found in having bigger houses, faster cars, louder hi-fis, the latest gadgets, more holidays. It seeks to convince us that it is in purchasing and using goods and services that we find our satisfaction, our happiness and our fulfilment.

This, of course, is patently untrue – indeed the irony and contradiction of the capitalist economy is that while it seeks to persuade us that our fulfilment and happiness depend on consuming, it actually requires us to become dissatisfied with what we have recently acquired, so that we feel the need to go out and purchase again. That contradiction, experienced by us again and again, helps to create the vacuum that exists in many people's lives today – a vacuum that they are encouraged to fill by yet further consumption! Yet despite the obvious untruth involved, the unspoken message that capitalism repeats again and again is that our happiness is dependent on our consumption of goods and services.

Security in Economic Assets

In itself, increasing the quantity and quality of the goods and services we consume is neutral (provided that it is not at the expense of others or of the environment, which in our Western economically developed world it unfortunately and obviously is).

What is to be challenged is the value that it imposes on us, namely that *our security is to be found in economic terms.* It seeks to persuade us that our security is to be sought in our assets, our properties, our bank balances. It seeks to persuade us that this is what guarantees our future security and the security of our children.

This, too, is patently untrue. A collapse in the property market in Ireland would see many families, who today live very comfortable lives, plunged into homelessness and poverty; a sharp rise in interest rates would put many families in Ireland, who today live very comfortable lives, into a debt situation from which they might not be able to escape. Yet, while we may realise that our accumulated assets are a very tenuous form of security, we are persuaded that there is nothing else that is more secure. The vacuum in many people's lives is further deepened by the belief imposed on us that the primary objective in life is to accumulate as much as we can.

Individualism

And so the third value of the capitalist system is *individualism.* The system promotes, encourages and rewards individual effort. The individual is the source of the innovation that drives capitalism, and the individual is the beneficiary of the rewards of capitalism. *My* security, therefore, is to be founded on the economic assets that I, *as an individual,* can accumulate. As the goods and services of this world are limited, then the struggle to find security in economic assets, *as individuals,* pushes us into a competitive struggle with other human beings, who become not the source of the fulfilment of our needs, but a threat to that fulfilment. The sense of individualism weakens the bonds that bind us together and seeks to deny the centrality of relationships to a fulfilled life.

Values of the Community of Jesus

The values of the new community inaugurated by Jesus are in direct contradiction to the values of individualism, consumerism and economic security proclaimed by capitalism.

Letting Go

It is in letting go, not in accumulating or holding on to, that we find our true happiness and our fulfilment. In letting go, we show our detachment from our material goods and our securities, a detachment that allows us to love God with all our heart and all our soul and all our mind (Matthew 22:37) and our neighbour in their need.

> How does God's love abide in anyone who has the world's goods and sees a brother or sister in need and yet refuses help?
> (1 John 3:17)

Security in Relationships

Our security is not to be found in our economic assets, which clearly, due to forces over which we may have little or no control, can be taken from us, literally overnight.

> Let the believer who is lowly boast in being raised up, and the rich in being brought low, because the rich will disappear like a flower in the field. For the sun rises with its scorching heat and withers the field; its flower falls, and its beauty perishes. It is the same way with the rich; in the midst of a busy life, they will wither away. (James 1:9-11)

Where does the Gospel tell us that our security is to be found? Security must be based on something that is unchanging and unchangeable. Otherwise it is not secure, it is built on sand. It can never, therefore, be based on economic assets. Our security is based only on the infinite and unconditional love of God. Our security is founded only on the knowledge that we are loved infinitely and unconditionally by God, a love that is unchanging and unchangeable.

Beloved, let us love one another, because love is from God; everyone who loves is born of God and knows God. Whoever does not love does not know God, for God is love. God's love was revealed among us in this way: God sent his only Son into the world so that we might live through him. In this is love, not that we loved God but that he loved us and sent his Son to be the atoning sacrifice for our sins. Beloved, since God loved us so much, we also ought to love one another. No one has ever seen God; if we love one another, God lives in us, and his love is perfected in us. (1 John 4:7-12)

Everyone wants to be loved. We, rightly, crave acceptance and belonging. Falling in love provides people with the most fulfilling experience of their lives. Wrapped in the arms of a boyfriend or girlfriend, two lovers wish that this moment of intense love might never end. They would not swap that moment for all the money in the world. Their happiest moments in life are in loving and being loved. But while nothing in life compares with the happiness of being in a relationship of love, the hope we have that that relationship might last for life is, unfortunately, often disappointed. If the fragile security we have is to be found in loving relationships, then our unchangeable security is to be found in the knowledge of the unconditional love of God for us. And how is that love mediated to us?

Relationships and Community

The love of God for us is mediated through community, through the love of others for us. Hence our true security is only to be found in community. It is in the solidarity with each other in community, in the relationships that we build with each other in community, that we find both fulfilment and security. In building the economic assets of the community, everyone finds security, both those who are able to contribute significantly to the building of those assets, as well as those who, through no fault of their own, are unable to do so. The assets we accumulate, we accumulate not for ourselves alone, but for the community.

Our solidarity with others impels us to share and to share radically.

> What good is it, my brothers and sisters, if you say you have faith but do not have works? Can faith save you? If a brother or sister is naked and lacks daily food, and one of you says to them, 'Go in peace; keep warm and eat your fill,' and yet you do not supply their bodily needs, what is the good of that? So faith by itself, if it has no works, is dead.
>
> But someone will say, 'You have faith and I have works.' Show me your faith apart from your works, and I by my works will show you my faith. (James 2:14-18)

As an individual, I cannot live the Gospel spirituality of letting go, except in community. As an individual, I can, of course, live a simple lifestyle: I can refuse to join the headlong rush to acquire more and bigger and better; I can be satisfied with having my basic needs met; I can reject the dominant values of the consumer society. But in living simply, no matter how good and valuable that is, I am not fundamentally challenging the values of this society. I am going in the same direction, only more slowly.

The spirituality of 'letting go' can only be lived in community, in solidarity with others. We, as community, can express our radical solidarity with each other through sharing what we have and who we are, and in that sharing present a value that is in contradiction to the values presented by our culture.

Letting Go – The Key to a Just World

How do we actually let go? How do we give back to God what God has already given to us? God has no need of what we possess. But others have. In this grossly unjust world, where 50 per cent of the population live on less than $2 per day, how can we give to those who are in dire poverty a standard of living that would enable them to live in a humane and dignified way? Our standard of living in the Western world has been created by economic growth (arguably built on slavery, colonialism and unjust trading relationships). If economic growth in our world were to increase to a point where it could enable everyone to enjoy our Western standard of living, we would destroy our planet with pollution and emissions. We simply cannot bring those in dire poverty up to anything like our standard of living, without us reducing our standard of living in the West. 'Letting go' is the spirituality of those who strive to build a more just world.

Young people today find an emptiness in their pursuit of individual wealth. They ask, 'What is the meaning of it all?' and cannot find an answer. What many do find meaningful and fulfilling is in giving to others, giving their time, giving their energy, giving themselves to make the lives of others a little less miserable, a little more meaningful. It is in giving that both the giver and the receiver find meaning.

Building a strong sense of community, a community that has the self-confidence to reach out and welcome into their midst the stranger, the immigrant and those on the margins, building a strong sense of solidarity with one another, is the direction in which we can seek to fill the vacuum created by the values that today's culture imposes on us.

People today are being pushed in a direction that is diametrically opposed to finding fulfilment and security – in the direction of individualism, isolation and aloneness. The Christian vision is that we belong to a community, the People of God. Many would say that I am an idealist, that I need to come back into the real world. In the real world in which we have to live and rear our family, what I am suggesting is pure nonsense, impossible to achieve, the unrealistic dreams of someone who lives in the clouds. And they are right. It is absurd. Just as absurd as looking at a child in the manger, utterly dependent on his parents for his well-being and even for his continued existence, and calling him All-Powerful God. Just as absurd as looking at a criminal hanging on a cross and calling him Infinite Goodness.

Conclusion

Jesus, the revelation of God, came into this world and lived amongst the people whom God had chosen to be the People of God. In return for their liberation from their oppressors in Egypt and the promise of continued protection by God, the People of God were to live as commanded by God, loving God and their neighbour. To help them, God gave them the Law, which instructed them how to worship the God who liberated them and how to live with each other in justice and peace.

But Jesus found a people amongst whom poverty and injustice was rife: the oppression from which God had rescued them was simply being repeated within the People of God, and the dignity of some of God's children was being denied to them by the way they were being rejected and marginalised within their society. Even worse, the Jewish authorities of his time interpreted the Law to suit their own purposes and used the Law itself to justify this oppression and injustice.

Jesus was appalled. What was happening was in contradiction to everything that God had expected from the People of God. Jesus' attempts, by both deed and word, to point out the infidelity of the leaders of the People of God was resisted at every turn and his constant criticism of those leaders led them to plot to get rid of him.

> They were looking for Jesus and were asking one another as they stood in the temple, 'What do you think? Surely he will

not come to the festival, will he?' Now the chief priests and the Pharisees had given orders that anyone who knew where Jesus was should let them know, so that they might arrest him. (John 11:56-57)

The rejection of Jesus by the leaders of the People of God led Jesus to establish the new People of God, the new community where God's will would be done. God's vision, the vision of Jesus, for this world was a place where everyone is cared for, everyone's needs are met, everyone is respected and valued. The gross inequalities, the injustice and marginalisation that now existed in the old community of God were to be abolished in the new community of God being inaugurated by Jesus. The new People of God was to be a community that lived by God's will and reflected God's vision for this world. This community was to be a 'light on a lamp-stand' (Matthew 5:14), showing the world how to live in peace and harmony; it was to be 'the salt of the world' (Matthew 5:13), the flavour in otherwise insipid food.

The Christian community is the new Community of God in our world today. If Jesus returned today, what would he say? Does the life of this community reflect the vision of God for our world? Or would Jesus find the same inequalities, injustice and marginalisation in this community as he once found two-thousand years ago? Does the Christian community reflect the same infidelity to God's will and vision as the Jewish community into which Jesus was born? Does the life of the Christian community, and the relationships within it, challenge the values and practices of the wider society in which it exists in a way that brings persecution and rejection from that society? Or does the Christian community sit comfortably in that society, indistinguishable from it? Have we betrayed the trust that God has placed in us? Have we rationalised away the Gospel to suit our own interests and comforts? Are we prepared for the radical conversion that would transform our relationships with each other, particularly with the poor and marginalised?

What is God's judgement on a world with so many living in obscene poverty while some few live in obscene wealth? Can God smile approvingly down on a world where millions live on the edge of starvation, or are condemned to death because they cannot afford a few cents to buy essential medicines? Could God live in a world where travellers are forced to live on the road-side, where people sleep in doorways, where those with disabilities cannot get essential services, where children with special needs wait years for assessment and even longer for help, without raising a voice in protest?

Jesus came to make the vision of God for our world a reality. To transform the world from where it is today to where God would like it to be tomorrow requires a revolution. That revolution is the community of Christians, which Jesus called the Kingdom, or Family, of God. We, that community, have a lot of soul-searching, a lot of hard thinking to do. We are called to listen long and hard to the Gospel, to the call of the King, who invites us to transform this world through a radical solidarity with all others, to follow him who gave his life for us by giving our own lives, and everything we have and are, for our brothers and sisters – a radical personal conversion that would revolutionise our world.

Jesus: Social Revolutionary? is an attempt to open a debate about the meaning of our faith and the obligations that belonging to the Christian community imposes on us. You can contribute to this debate by sharing your views and reflections with the author and others on www.jcfj.ie/jesussocialrevolutionary